Original Hessisch
The Best of Hessian Food

Ess un drink,
dann wächster aach dei Blomm om Hout!

Hessisches Sprichwort

Eat and drink, and the flower
on your hat will keep growing!

Hessian Proverb

HÄDECKE

Angela Francisca Endress · Barbara Nickerson

Original Hessisch
The Best of
Hessian Food

4 3 2 1 | 2010 2011 2012 2013

© 2010 Walter Hädecke Verlag, Weil der Stadt
www.haedecke-verlag.de

Rezeptbearbeitung und Texte: Barbara Nickerson
Übersetzung ins Englische: Lyra Wagner
Foodfotografie, Styling und
Vorsatzmotive: Angela Francisca Endress
Food: Marion Dietz
Bildnachweis Seite 82/83: Andrew Chambers/istockphoto (rechte Seite, oben rechts), Claudia Dewald/istockphoto (linke Seite, oben links), Jeremy Edwards/istockphoto (rechte Seite, Mitte), Gesellschaft für Rheingauer Weinkultur mbH, Eltville (linke Seite, obere Bildzeile Mitte und rechts, zweite Zeile links, untere Bildzeile, rechte Seite oben und unten links), Oleg Prikhodko/istockphoto (linke Seite, zweite Bildzeile rechts), Frank Rotthaus/istockphoto (rechte Seite, oben Mitte), Andreas Weber/istockphoto (linke Seite, dritte Bildzeile und rechte Seite, unten rechts)
Gestaltung Umschlag, Vorsatz und Seite 82/83: Julia Graff, Design & Produktion, Stuttgart
Typographie und Satz: ES Typo-Graphic, Ellen Steglich, Stuttgart
Reproduktion: LUP AG, Köln
Druck: Westermann Druck Zwickau

Recipes and texts editor: Barbara Nickerson
English translation: Lyra Wagner
Food Photographs, styling and endpapers' pictures: Angela Francisca Endress
Food: Marion Dietz
Pictures page 82/83: Andrew Chambers/istockphoto (right page, first line on the right), Claudia Dewald/istockphoto (left page, first line on the left), Jeremy Edwards/istockphoto (right page in the middle), Gesellschaft für Rheingauer Weinkultur mbH, Eltville (left page, first line in the middle and on the right, second line on the left and last line, right page, first line on the left and last line at the left), Oleg Prikhodko/istockphoto (left page, second line on the right), Frank Rotthaus/istockphoto (right page, first line in the middle), Andreas Weber/istockphoto (left page, third line and right page, last line on the right)
Cover, endpapers and page 82/83 design: Julia Graff, Design & Production, Stuttgart
Typography and typesetting: ES Typo-Graphic, Ellen Steglich, Stuttgart
Reproductions: LUP AG, Cologne
Printing: Westermann Druck Zwickau

ISBN 978-3-7750-0583-8

Printed in Germany 2010

Danksagung

Vom Norden bis zum Süden haben uns viele Gastwirte, Köche und Familien ihre hauseigenen Rezepte zur Verfügung gestellt. Dafür bedanken wir uns herzlich, besonders bei:

Emmi Anders, Iris und Thomas Arnhold, Helga Bachmann, Dr. Peter Becker, Else Benner (Vorsitzende Landfrauenverein Griesheim), Ursula Curth, Matthias Fleischmann (www.rebstock-steinbach.de), Helma Goldbach, Hilde Gromes, Ursula Heimes (www.saalburg.de), Lotti Henrici (Gaststätte „Zum Deutschen Haus" Usingen-Eschbach), Helga Hettler, Herbert Hettler, Bärbel Höhenberger, Lilli Holl, Klaus Hottmann, Hans-Jost Knauf, Kai Uwe Korn (Kochen & Kommunikation, www.le-kuk.de), Susanne Lengemann-Kampe, Sylvia Michels (www.hessenpark.de), Heinz Peter, Beate Plohmer, Brigitte Rückauf, Berta Schmidt, Hubert Schmidt, Ingrid Schmidt, Manfred Seuss (www.kaesehaus-hessenpark.de), Monika Trost, Barbara Viehl-Stern, Martin Vollmar, Bettina Wagner (Kornbrennerei Gerhard Wagner, Dauborn), Katja Zöller (www.kaufhaushessen.de) sowie bei www.saenger-eschbach.de und bei www.heimatruhe-afe.de.

Abkürzungen und Maße

kg	– Kilogramm
g	– Gramm
l	– Liter
Msp.	– Messerspitze | 1 Msp. entspricht ca. 2 g
ml	– Milliliter = 0,001 Liter
EL	– Esslöffel | 1 EL entspricht ca. 15 ml
TL	– Teelöffel | 1 TL entspricht ca. 5 ml
Bd.	– Bund | 1 Prise entspricht ca. 0,5 g
P.	Päckchen

Die Rezepte sind – soweit nicht anders angegeben – für 4 Portionen.

Abbreviations and Measurements

lbs(s)	– pound(s)
fl oz	– fluid ounce(s)
pt(s)	– pint(s)
tbsp(s)	– tablespoon(s)
tsp(s)	– teaspoon(s)

1 cup is approx. ½ pint (Am.) which is approx. ¼ quart. 1 tbsp is about ½ fl oz. 1 tsp is about 1/5 fl oz. 1 pinch is about 1/8 teaspoon.

If not otherwise indicated, the recipes yield 4 servings.

Rezepte

Recipes

Seit jeher gelten die Hessen als weltoffen. Fremde Einflüsse sorgten über die Jahrhunderte bis heute für ein geistig reges Klima, das auf die zentrale Lage in der Mitte Deutschlands und auf die guten Verkehrswege zurückzuführen ist, die als alte Handelsrouten teilweise frühgeschichtlichen Ursprung haben. Hessen nimmt heute eine Spitzenstellung ein, denn es gilt als führendes Wirtschaftszentrum Deutschlands und sogar als eine der dynamischsten Regionen Europas. Wirtschaftlicher Mittelpunkt ist das Rhein-Main-Gebiet mit den Städten Frankfurt, Offenbach, Wiesbaden und Darmstadt. Im Raum Kassel und im Lahn-Dill-Kreis entwickelten sich nach dem Zweiten Weltkrieg starke Industriestandorte. Bildung und Wissenschaft wurden schon zu Beginn der Christianisierung gepflegt, was vor allem den Benediktinermönchen und den zahlreichen Klöstern zu verdanken ist, die hier angesiedelt wurden. Heute wird an fünf Universitäten gelehrt und geforscht.

Geografisch liegen im Norden Hessens die klimatisch rauen Höhenzüge von Rheinhardswald, Habichtswald und Kaufunger Wald. Viele kennen den Vogelsberg als schlafenden Vulkan, den Hohen Meißner und das Knüllgebirge. Im Westen – zur Lahn, Dill und zur Sieg hin – erstreckt sich das Rheinische Schiefergebirge. Weiter südlich liegen die Berglandschaften von Westerwald, Taunus, Odenwald und Spessart. Das Land besitzt einige beckenartige Senken wie das Kinzigtal, das Werratal oder das Fuldaer Becken.

Die großen Waldgebiete und die Fülle an heilenden Mineralquellen zeichnen Hessen ganz besonders aus. In mehr als 30 mondänen bis romantischen Heil- und Kurorten wie Wiesbaden, Bad Homburg oder Bad Nauheim finden Gäste Entspannung und Erholung. Ausgesprochen fröhlich und mit viel „Gebabbel" geht es im südlichen Teil, in den Weinbaugebieten der Bergstraße und des Rheingaus zu, wo wegen des günstigen Klimas im Hessischen Ried auch Spargel angebaut wird.

Wer der hessischen Küche nachspüren will, findet sie in den typischen Ebbelwoi-Wirtschaften und in zahlreichen Landgasthöfen, die traditionelle Gerichte anbieten. Deftige Hausmannskost wie „Rippsche mit Kraut", „Grie Sooß", „Handkäs' mit Mússik" und dazu ein hauseigener Ebbelwoi (oder Stöffche, wie der Frankfurter zum Apfelwein sagt) „dun Leib un Seel sammehalle". Derb und herzlich ist der Hesse: Ein gutes Lokal lobt er wegen seiner großen Portionen mit „Rummsticker" oder „Kodledder", groß wie „en Abtrittsdeckel". Die nordhessische Küche bestand früher aus einfachen Speisen, denn magere Ernten brachten oft Armut und nicht viel zum Essen hervor. Im Süden war durch milderes Klima und den Einfluss der Römer sowie später der Franzosen stets mehr Raffinesse zu finden. Heute wie damals wird Gastfreundschaft in Hessen großgeschrieben. Was fordert mehr auf, ordentlich zuzulangen, als die Einladung der „Madam" (wie „de Babba" seine Frau liebevoll nennt): „Was mer uff de Disch stelle, gewwe mer verlorn"?

Auf den hessischen Speisezetteln stehen Gerichte mit unergründlichen Namen wie Storzeniere, Wetzstahkließ oder Krautshäubchen. So unterschiedlich wie die Menschen in Hessen von Norden bis Süden sind, so unterschiedlich schmecken auch ihre Gerichte. Seit eh und je schwört jede Familie auf ihr eigenes, ursprüngliches, hessisches Rezept. Weil es unmöglich ist, allen Hessen ins „Kochdippche zu gugge", bieten die Rezepte in diesem Buch einen Querschnitt aus dem großen Repertoire von hessischen Gastwirten, Köchen und Familien. Wir danken es ihnen, dass sie uns ihre hauseigenen Rezepte und so manche Geschichten und Tricks verraten haben. Und jetzt: „Gude Abbedidd, nix verschlabbert un nix verschütt!"

For centuries, Hesse has been known as a cosmopolitan place. Outside influences have ensured an intellectually open minded climate that can be felt to this day. This is due to its central location in the middle of Germany, as well as to the good transportation connections which often date back to early history when they served as trade routes. Today, Hesse is one of Germany's top federal states. It counts as a leading financial centre and is considered one of the most dynamic regions in Europe. Its economic centre is the Rhein-Main region, home to the cities of Frankfurt, Offenbach, Wiesbaden and Darmstadt. The areas around Kassel and Lahn-Dill County developed to become seats of industry after the Second World War. Education and science have always been cultivated in Hesse and can be traced back to the early period of Christianization. In particular, this was thanks to the Benedictine monks and the numerous abbeys that settled here. These days, no less than five universities teach and conduct research in the region.

Geographically speaking, northern Hesse has a rough climate and is covered by a range of hills that is home to the Rheinhardswald, Habichtswald and Kaufunger Wald forests. The Vogelsberg, a dormant volcano, is well known, as are the Hoher Meißner and the Knüllgebirge. To the west, the Rheinish Slate Range stretches out in the direction of the Lahn, Dill and Sieg. Further south lay the hilly regions of Westerwald, Taunus, Odenwald and Spessart. The state of Hesse also has a number of basin-like depressions, such as the Kinzigtal, the Werratal and the Fulda basin.

The large forested areas and a multitude of healing mineral water springs distinguish the State of Hesse especially. Guests can relax and convalesce in more than 30 spas and sanatoriums, ranging from the fashionable to the romantic, in places like Wiesbaden, Bad Homburg or Bad Nauheim. The people in the south, in the vineyard regions along the Bergstrasse and the Rheingau, are known for their particular cheerfulness and their "*Gebabbel*" or "chatter". In Ried, the climate is mild enough to grow asparagus.

A visitor searching for real Hessian cuisine, will find it in the typical *Ebbelwoi-Wirtschaften* and numerous country inns that serve traditional dishes. Hearty country fare like pork loin with cabbage, green herb's sauce, hand cheese with "music" and homebrewed apple cider (or *Stöffche*, as it is known in Frankfurt) are said to "keep body and soul together". The people of Hesse are rough but cordial.

A good inn earns its reputation with large helpings of Rumpsteak, or cutlets the size of a pillow. Food in northern Hesse used to consist of simple meals. Poor harvests often resulted in poverty and provided little to eat. In contrast, the mild climate of the south together with the influence of the Romans, and later the French, meant that the food was always more sophisticated. Today, as always, hospitality plays an important part in Hesse's culture. What better invitation to enjoy a hearty meal than *Madam's* (as the *Babba*, father of the family, affectionately calls his wife) saying, "Eat up, whatever's on the table is lost to us!" (meant with a certain irony). Unfathomable names like Storzeniere, Wetzstahlkließ or Krautshäubchen can be found on menus throughout Hesse, and just as there are differences between the people of the North and the South there are differences in their food. For as long as anyone can remember, each individual family has sworn by their own original Hessian recipes. Since it's impossible to look over the shoulder of every cook in Hesse, the recipes contained within this book offer a wide selection from the enormous range of recipes used by restaurants, cooks and families. Our thanks to all of them for sharing their own personal recipes, and for the stories and tips that they provided. And now: Enjoy your meal, don't dribble, and don't spill anything!

Frankfurter Linsensuppe mit Würstchen
Frankfurt Style Lentil soup with Sausages

Rheingauer Sauerampfersuppe
Rheingauer Sorrel soup

Frankfurter Linsensuppe mit Würstchen

1 Tasse Tellerlinsen
2 EL Öl
1 Zwiebel
1 Scheibe Speck
1 Karotte
1 Stück Sellerieknolle
4 Paar Frankfurter Würstchen
2 Kartoffeln
etwas gekörnte Gemüsebrühe
Salz, Pfeffer
Petersilie
Weißweinessig
Wasser

2 EL Öl in einem großen Topf erhitzen und die gewürfelte Zwiebel und den gewürfelten Speck darin glasig dünsten. Karotte und Sellerieknolle dazugeben und mitbraten. Die vorher, falls nötig, in warmem Wasser eingeweichten Linsen samt Einweichwasser zu dem Wurzelgemüse geben, ca. 1 Liter Wasser und etwas Gemüsebrühe zum Würzen dazugeben und ca. 25 Minuten köcheln lassen. Ab und zu umrühren und bei Bedarf mit etwas Wasser begießen. Dann die gewürfelten Kartoffeln in die Linsensuppe geben und weitere 10 Minuten köcheln lassen. Mit den Gewürzen, der Petersilie und Essig abschmecken. Zwischendurch die Frankfurter Würstchen in Wasser heiß werden lassen, nicht kochen, damit sie nicht aufplatzen. Die heißen „Werschtcher" mit mittelscharfem Senf getrennt zur Suppe servieren.

Grüne Bohnensuppe mit Milch

8 Teller
500 g Grüne Bohnen
    (auch Schnippelbohnen genannt)
2 mittelgroße Kartoffeln
½ l Gemüsebrühe (Rezept S. 80)
1 TL Salz
1½ l Milch
Pfeffer

Die grünen Bohnen waschen, abtropfen, gipfeln (evtl. Fäden abziehen) und in mundgerechte Stücke schnippeln. Kartoffeln waschen, schälen und in Würfel schneiden. Kartoffeln und Bohnen in der Gemüsebrühe in ca. 20 Minuten gar kochen. Milch dazugeben, aufkochen und mit Salz und Pfeffer abschmecken.

Anmerkung

Ein Zweiglein Bohnenkraut, während des Kochens zugefügt, verfeinert den Geschmack.
Steht die Suppe etwas länger, bildet sich eine Milchhaut, die vor dem Servieren abgeschöpft wird.

Rezept von Katja Zöller, Frankfurt

Rezept von Emmi Anders, Taunus

Frankfurt Style Lentil soup with Sausages

1 cup of Puy lentils
2 tbsps oil
1 thick slice of smoked bacon
1 onion
1 carrot
1 piece of celeriac root
4 pairs of Frankfurter sausages
2 potatoes
a little roughly strained vegetable stock
salt
pepper
parsley
white wine vinegar
water

Heat 2 tbsps of oil in a large saucepan and sweat the onions with the diced bacon until clear.
Add the carrot and celeriac root. Pour in the pre-soaked lentils with the water they were soaked in with 1¾ pints of water and a little vegetable stock for flavor. Simmer for about 25 minutes. Once in a while give everything a stir an add a little water if necessary.
Add the diced potatoes to the lentilsoup and simmer for a further 10 minutes. Season with parsley, salt and pepper, and vinegar.
Meanwhile, warm the Frankfurter sausages in hot water. Be careful not to let them boil, or they will burst.
Serve the hot sausages with medium hot mustard as an accompaniment to the soup.

Recipe by Katja Zöller, Frankfurt

Green Bean Soup with Milk

8 bowls
1 lb green beans (also known "Schnippel-bohnen" or snipping beans)
2 medium sized potatoes
1 pt vegetable stock (page 81)
1 tsp salt
3 pts milk
pepper

Wash and drain the green beans, then top and tail them. Remove any strings and cut into bite-sized pieces. Wash, peel and dice the potatoes. Cook the potatoes and the beans in the vegetable stock for approx. 20 minutes. Add the milk. Bring to the boil, and season with salt and pepper.

Note
A sprig of savory in the stock refines the flavor. If left to stand, the soup forms a skin which should be removed before serving.

Recipe by Emmi Anders, Taunus

Zwiebelsalat
Onion Salad

Rheingauer Sauerampfersuppe

250 g frischer Sauerampfer
125 g Kopfsalat
　30 g Butter
375 ml Gemüsebrühe (Rezept S. 80)
500 ml Sahne
125 ml Rheingauer Riesling, Spätlese
　3 Eigelbe
　2 Scheiben Weißbrot
　1 Knoblauchzehe

Sauerampfer und Kopfsalat putzen, waschen und in Streifen schneiden. Butter heiß werden lassen und ¾ des Sauerampfers und den Kopfsalat darin kurz andünsten. Gemüsebrühe und Sahne zufügen (3 EL der Sahne zurückbehalten). Alles heiß werden lassen. Den Riesling zufügen und kurz vor dem Kochen den Topf von der Kochstelle nehmen. Eigelbe mit Sahne verrühren und unter die Suppe ziehen, sodass sie schön bindet. Nochmals alles erwärmen, die Suppe soll aber nicht mehr kochen. Weißbrot in Würfel schneiden und in der Pfanne rösten. Knoblauch schälen, dazugeben und kurz mit anrösten. Die Brotwürfel auf die angerichtete Suppe geben und mit dem restlichen Sauerampfer dekorieren.

Anmerkung
Kopfsalat wird im Rheingau gerne als Gemüsegarnitur kurz mitgedünstet oder klein geschnitten frisch mit warmen Speisen angerichtet.

Tipp
Gibt es keinen Sauerampfer, ersetzen ihn die Rheingauer gerne mit jungen Brennnesseln.

Zwiebelsalat

3 dicke Gemüsezwiebeln
3 EL Essigessenz
3 EL Zucker
3 EL Wasser
1 saurer Apfel (z. B. Granny Smith)
250 g Mayonnaise (Rezept S. 50)
　1 Becher Schmand (200 g)
Salz
Pfeffer

Die Zwiebeln schälen, halbieren und in feine Monde schneiden. Essigessenz, Zucker und warmes Wasser verrühren und über die Zwiebeln geben. Einen Tag ziehen lassen. Dann den Zwiebelsaft abgießen. Den Apfel entkernen, in kleine Würfel schneiden und zu den Zwiebelmonden geben. Mayonnaise mit Schmand verrühren und untermischen. Mit Salz und Pfeffer abschmecken. Einige Stunden ziehen lassen und erneut abschmecken.
Dazu passen Ofen- oder Pellkartoffeln.

Anmerkung
Im Bereich Biedenkopf wird dem Brauch des Kartoffelbratens im Altweibersommer gefrönt; überall werden in der Glut der heruntergebrannten offenen Feuer Kartoffeln gegart. Dazu gehört auch der „Zwiebelsalat Hinterländer Art", eine schnellere Version: 2 dicke Gemüsezwiebeln, 2 Becher Schmand, 1 EL Weißweinessig, 1 EL Mayonnaise, Pfeffer, Salz. Gemüsezwiebeln klein schneiden und 2 Minuten abkochen. Anschließend mit kaltem Wasser abschrecken. Aus allen Zutaten eine Marinade anrühren, die abgekochten Zwiebeln dazugeben und gut durchrühren. 1 Stunde ziehen lassen.

Rezept von Kai Uwe Korn, Eltville

Rezepte von Martin Vollmar, Marburger Land

Rheingauer Sorrel soup

8 oz fresh sorrel
4 oz lettuce
1½ oz butter
3 cups of vegetable stock (page 81)
1 pt cream
½ cup white wine – preferably Rheingauer
    Riesling, Spätlese
3 egg yolks
2 slices of white bread
1 clove of garlic

Clean and wash the sorrel and the lettuce, then cut into strips. Heat the butter and fry ¾ of the sorrel together with the lettuce. Add the vegetable stock and the cream (keep 3 tbsps of the cream for later) and heat through. Pour in the wine, and just before the soup begins to boil remove it from the heat. Beat the egg yolks and the remaining cream. Stir into the soup until it thickens. Return to the heat, but do not allow to boil.
Cut the white bread into cubes and fry in the pan. Peel the garlic and fry it in the pan with the bread. Fry a little. Garnish the soup with the bread croutons and the remaining sorrel leaves.

Comment

In the Rheingau, lettuce is often served braised as a vegetable side serving, or finely chopped and served fresh as an accompaniment to warm meals.

Tip

If you cannot get hold of sorrel, then in Rheingau they like to use young nettles as a substitute.

Recipe by Kai Uwe Korn, Eltville

Onion Salad

3 large Spanish onions
3 tbsps vinegar essence
3 tbsps sugar
3 tbsps water
1 sour tasting apple (e. g. Granny Smith)
approx. 1 cup of mayonnaise (page 51)
1 pot of heavy sour cream (approx. 7 fl oz)
salt
pepper

Peel and halve the onions. Slice each half lengthways into 8 pieces. Mix the vinegar essence, sugar and warm water and pour over the finely cut moon shaped onion slices. Leave to marinate for 1 day. Drain off the liquid. Core and dice the apple and add it to the onions.
Mix the mayonnaise and the heavy sour cream and fold in the onions. Season to taste, with salt and pepper. Allow to marinate for a few hours and season again.
Best served with baked or jacket potatoes.

Comment

In late summer in the region around Biedenkopf, it is traditional to bake potatoes in the embers of summer bonfires. Traditionally, they are served with another onion salad, which is quicker to make, called "Zwiebelsalat Hinterländer Art"

2 large Spanish onions
2 pots of heavy cream (approx. 2 cups)
1 tbsp white wine vinegar
1 tbsp mayonnaise
pepper, salt

Slice the onions finely and boil them for two minutes. Afterwards plunge them in cold water and drain well. Use the remaining ingredients to make the marinade. Add the blanched onions and mix well. Leave to stand for one hour.

Recipes by Martin Vollmar, Marburger Land

Spargel-Eier-Salat
Asparagus & Egg Salad

Spargel-Eier-Salat

500 g weiße Spargelköpfe
Salzwasser
 3 Eier, hart gekocht
 1 Schalotte
2–3 Zweiglein Dill
 1 TL mittelscharfer Senf
 1 EL Branntweinessig
Salz
 3 EL Rapsöl
Zucker
weißer Pfeffer

Spargel waschen und in Salzwasser 8–10 Minuten kochen, sodass der Spargel noch bissfest ist. Herausnehmen und abkühlen lassen. Die Eier schälen und in Scheiben schneiden.

Für die Marinade die Schalotte in feine Würfel schneiden, Dill waschen, Spitzen abzupfen und klein schneiden. Senf mit Essig, Salz und Pfeffer verrühren und das Öl nach und nach unterschlagen. Zucker und Dill zufügen und nochmals abschmecken. Marinade über den Spargel geben, Eierscheiben vorsichtig unterheben und ca. 30 Minuten durchziehen lassen.

Abwandlung

In die Marinade ein hart gekochtes Eigelb unterrühren und das hart gekochte Eiweiß fein gehackt dazugeben. Sehr hübsch sieht es aus, wenn der Spargelsalat auf Salatblättern angerichtet wird.

Anmerkung

Bei Spargelköpfen entfällt das Schälen, sodass gar kein Abfall entsteht. Als Vorspeise kann gekochter Schinken in Streifen unter den Salat gegeben werden. Als feines Hauptgericht an heißen Tagen wird der Salat mit Salzkartoffeln und einem kleinen Schweineschnitzel serviert.

Tipp

Aus der Spargelbrühe eine gesunde Spargelsuppe kochen. Einfach eine helle Mehlschwitze aus 50 g Mehl und 60 g Butter bereiten und mit 1 Liter Spargelbrühe auffüllen. Nach Geschmack einen Schuss Sahne unterrühren.

Rezept von Else Benner, Griesheim

Asparagus & Egg Salad

1 lb white asparagus tips
water
salt
3 hard boiled eggs
1 shallot
2–3 sprigs of dill
1 tsp medium hot mustard
1 tbsp brandy vinegar
salt
3 tbsps rapeseed oil
sugar
white pepper

Wash the asparagus and cook in salt water for about 8–10 minutes so that it is still firm to the bite. Drain and leave to cool. Peel the boiled eggs and cut them into slices.

For the marinade, finely dice the shallots. Wash the dill, remove the tips and chop finely. Mix the mustard, vinegar, salt and pepper together, then beat in the oil bit by bit. Add the sugar and dill. Season to taste.
Pour the marinade over the asparagus. Carefully fold in the egg slices and leave to marinate for about 30 minutes.

Variation

Stir the yolk of a hard boiled egg into the marinade and then add the finely chopped egg white. The asparagus salad looks very attractive when served on a bed of lettuce.

Comment

If you use asparagus tips there is no need to peel them, so there are no scraps.

For an ideal starter, add thin strips of ham to the salad.

For a main course on a hot day, serve with boiled potatoes and a small schnitzel.

Tip

Use the water from cooking the asparagus to make a healthy asparagus soup.
Simply make a roux sauce using 2 oz of plain flour and approx. 2½ oz of butter for every 2 pints of asparagus stock.
Add a dash of cream to taste.

Recipe by Else Benner, Griesheim

Schbannschlauch/Griewerchsgmies
Spanish Leeks

Schbannschlauch/ Griewerchsgmies

1 kg Lauch/Porree
1 l Gemüsebrühe (Rezept S. 80)
100 g Dörrfleisch (durchwachsener
    Räucherspeck)
10 g Butter
2 Scheiben Vollkorntoast

Lauch gründlich putzen, die sehr dunklen, oberen Enden abschneiden. Die Stangen in fingerlange Stücke schneiden und in der Brühe ca. 20 Minuten bissfest garen. Dörrfleisch in Würfel schneiden, knusprig anbraten, aus der Pfanne nehmen. Vollkorntoast toasten, in Würfel schneiden, in der Pfanne die Butter erhitzen und die Toastwürfel darin kross braten. Lauch gut abtropfen lassen, anrichten und die Dörrfleisch- und Toastwürfel darüber geben. Heiß servieren.

Anmerkung

Spanischer Lauch ist eine Sortengruppe des aus dem Mittelmeerraum stammenden Ackerlauchs. Dieses Gemüse zählt zur Gattung Allium in der Familie der Lauchgewächse (Alliaceae). In Nordhessen wurde der Begriff mundartlich abgerundet und so entstand daraus „Schbannschlauch". Das Gericht wird in ganz Nordhessen zubereitet, in Kassel als „Schbannschlauch", in der Schwalm als „Griewerchsgmies".

Rezept von Klaus Hottmann, Schwalm

Warmer Lattch (Salat)

1 Kopfsalat (Lattch)
100 g Dörrfleisch (durchwachsener
    Räucherspeck)
1 EL Mehl
1 EL Essig
5 EL Schmand
1 Eigelb

Vom „Lattch" die Blätter ablösen, waschen und gut abtropfen lassen oder in einem Küchentuch oder einer Salatschleuder trocken schleudern. Dörrfleisch in Würfel schneiden, in einer Pfanne anbraten, Mehl darüberstreuen und in dem Fett kurz andünsten. Essig dazugeben und unter kräftigem Rühren zusammen aufkochen lassen. Dabei sollte eine glatte Masse ohne Klümpchen entstehen. Von der Kochstelle nehmen, Schmand unterrühren und Eigelb darunterziehen. Die Marinade nochmals heiß werden lassen, nicht mehr kochen. Die heiße Soße über den Salat geben und sofort servieren.

Anmerkung

Seit 1728 feiern die Schwälmer alljährlich 14 Tage nach Pfingsten ihre Salatkirmes in Ziegenhain, dem Zentrum des Schwälmer Landes. Das Heimatfest erinnert an jenen Tag, an dem Landgraf Karl die Schwälmer Bauern von der Notwendigkeit des Kartoffelanbaus überzeugen wollte und sie zu einem Kartoffel- und Salatessen nach Ziegenhain einlud. Neu Hinzugezogene bekommen heute auf der Festbühne einen Kopfsalat an den Arm gebunden, werden hochgehoben und damit allen vorgezeigt: „Er wird gelattcht" heißt es. Auf diese Weise findet die Eingemeindung der Ziegenhainer statt.

Rezept von Hans-Jost Knauf, Schwalm

Spanish Leeks

2 lbs leeks
2 pts of vegetable stock (page 81)
4 oz streaky smoked bacon
approx. ½ oz butter
2 slices of whole-wheat toast

Clean the leeks thoroughly and cut off the very dark ends.
Cut the stalks into finger length pieces and cook them in the stock for 20 minutes or until firm to the bite.
Dice the bacon, fry until crispy and remove from the pan. Toast and then dice the bread. Heat the butter in the pan and fry the bread until crunchy. Drain the leeks well and arrange on a plate. Cover with bacon and croutons. Serve warm.

Comment

The Spanish leek is a variety of broad leaf or wild leek which originally comes from the region around the Mediterranean. It belongs to the Allium genera which is a member of the Alliaceae family.
In Northern Hesse, the name became part of the local vocabulary and changed to become "Schbannschlauch".
This meal is prepared all over Hesse. In Kassel it is known as "Schbannschlauch", in the region of Schwalm it is known as "Griewerchsgmies".

Recipe by Klaus Hottmann, Schwalm

Warm Lettuce Salad

1 lettuce
4 oz smoked streaky bacon
1 tbsp flour
1 tbsp vinegar
5 tbsps heavy sour cream
1 egg yolk

Separate the lettuce leaves. Wash and drain them well, or dry them in a tea towel or salad spinner. Dice the bacon and fry gently in a pan. Sprinkle with flour, and brown. Add the vinegar and bring to the boil, stirring quickly to form a smooth paste with no lumps. Remove from the heat and stir in the heavy sour cream and egg yolk. Reheat the marinade, but do not let it boil. Pour the hot sauce over the salad and serve immediately.

Comment

Since 1728, every year, the people of Schwalm have celebrated the Schwalmer Salad Festival. It takes place 14 days after Pentecost, in Ziegenhain, the centre of Schwalmerland. The town festival, or "Heimatfest", commemorates the day on which Landgraf Karl attempted to convince the people of Schwalm of the importance of planting potatoes, by inviting them to a feast of potatoes and salad in Ziegenhain. To this day, new members of the community have a lettuce tied to their arm onstage and are carried up in the air and shown off to the crowd. This is a rite of passage which introduces new members of the village to the rest of the community – they call it "Lattaching".

Recipe by Hans-Jost Knauf, Schwalm

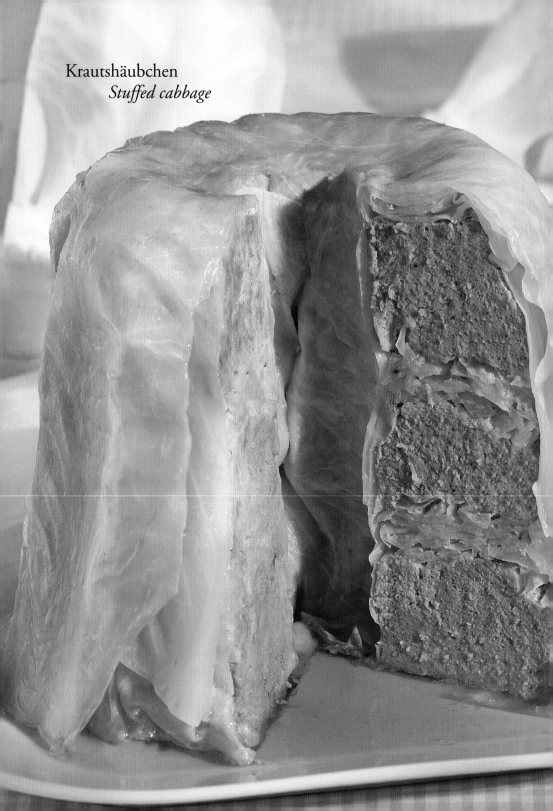

Krautshäubchen
Stuffed cabbage

Krautshäubchen

6 Portionen

1 großer Kopf Weißkraut
3 l Wasser
1 TL Salz, ½ TL Kümmel
etwas Bohnenkraut
etwas Muskat
1 kg Hackfleisch, vom Schwein oder Rind
1 EL Tomatenmark, 1 EL Senf
1 EL Salz, 1 EL Pfeffer
Puddingform mit Deckel
 (2½ l Fasungsvermögen)
etwas Butter für die Form

Béchamelsoße

1 kleine Zwiebel
90 g Butter, 100 g Mehl
1 l von der Kohlbrühe

Vom Weißkraut 7 ganze Blätter ablösen, den Rest
in Streifen hobeln. Wasser mit den Gewürzen
zum Kochen bringen, erst die ganzen Kohlblätter,
dann die Streifen darin blanchieren. Herausnehmen,
abtropfen und die Brühe zur Seite stellen. Hackfleisch mit Tomatenmark, Senf, Salz und Pfeffer
würzen. Die Form buttern, mit den Kohlblättern
auslegen und diese über den Rand hängen lassen.
Krautstreifen und Hackfleisch abwechselnd hinein
schichten. Die überhängenden Blätter als Abschluss
darüberschlagen. Die Puddingform verschließen.
In ein Wasserbad stellen, zum Kochen bringen
und ca. 1 Stunde garen.
Für die Soße die Zwiebel fein hacken, in heißer
Butter glasig dünsten, Mehl zufügen. Unter Rühren
eine helle Einbrenne zubereiten, mit der Kohlbrühe
aufgießen und zur glatten Soße rühren. Ca. 10
Minuten köcheln lassen. Das Krautshäubchen aus
der Puddingform stürzen, Soße dazu servieren.

Rezept von Helga Bachmann, Nordhessen

Solberfleisch

800 g gutes Kochfleisch/Siedfleisch vom Rind
 (Bürgermeisterstück, Bug oder Brustkern)
250 g Pökelsalz
 2 l Wasser

Aus Pökelsalz und kaltem Wasser eine Lake herstellen. Wenn sich das Salz aufgelöst hat, das
Fleisch so einlegen, dass es überall gut mit Wasser
bedeckt ist. Sechs Tage darin pökeln.
Zur Zubereitung das Fleisch herausnehmen, in
einen Topf legen und mit frischem kalten Wasser
auffüllen, sodass es bedeckt ist. Einmal kurz aufkochen und dann bei ca. 70 °C etwa 2 Stunden
sieden lassen. Darauf achten, dass es keinesfalls
kocht, sonst wird das Fleisch zäh.
Zu dem aufgeschnittenen Fleisch serviert der Hesse Meerrettichsoße (Seite 30), Wirsing (Seite 30)
oder Grie Sooß (Seite 50) und auf jeden Fall Salzkartoffeln.

Anmerkung

Der Name kommt von Sulper (Salpeter), der frü-
her zum Pökeln, also Konservieren von Fleisch und
Wurst, benutzt wurde.
Die Hüftspitze vom Rind heißt Bürgermeisterstück,
weil sich das gute Stück früher außer dem hohen
Herrn niemand leisten konnte.

Rezept von Brigitte Rückauf, Taunus

Stuffed cabbage

6 servings
1 large white cabbage, 6 pints of water
1 tsp salt, ½ tsp caraway
some savory, a little nutmeg
4 lbs minced/ground meat, pork or beef
1 tbsp tomato paste, 1 tbsp mustard
1 tsp salt, 1 tsp pepper
1 pt dessert mold with a lid (5 pts volume)
a little butter to grease

Béchamel Sauce
3 oz butter, 4 oz flour
1 small onion, 2 pts cabbage stock

Loosen 7 leaves (whole) from the cabbage and shred the rest into strips. Bring the water and the seasoning to the boil and blanch the cabbage leaves. Then blanch the shredded cabbage. Remove from the water and drain. Keep the cabbage stock for later. Season the meat with the tomato paste, mustard, salt and pepper. Grease the mold and line it with the whole cabbage leaves, allowing the leaves to hang over the rim. Fill the mold with alternate layers of shredded cabbage and meat until full. Fold the overhanging leaves over the filling and seal the mold with the lid.
Place in a pot of hot water (bainmarie) and bring to the boil. Cook for approximately 1 hour.
For the béchamel sauce, finely chop the onions and glaze in hot butter. Sprinkle with flour to form a light roux. Slowly add the cabbage stock stirring constantly to form a smooth sauce. Simmer for about 10 minutes.
Turn the "Krautshäubchen" out of the mold and serve with the sauce.

Recipe by Helga Bachmann, Nordhessen

Boiled Pickled Beef

1¾ lbs good quality boiling beef ("Bürgermeis-
    terstück", shoulder or brisket)
8 oz pickling salt
4 pts water

Dissolve the pickling salt in cold water to make the brine. Once the salt has dissolved, place the meat in the brine so that the surface of the meat is well covered with liquid. Leave to pickle for 6 days.
Remove the meat and place it in a saucepan, then fill the pan with cold water, so that the surface of the meat is covered. Bring the water the boil, and then reduce the heat and leave to simmer at approx. 160 °F for 2 hours. Be sure not to let the water boil or the meat will be tough.
In Hesse, slices of the meat are served with horseradish sauce (page 51), Savoy Cabbage (page 51) or Green Sauce (page 31), and always with boiled potatoes.

Comment

The German name "Solberfleisch" comes from the word "sulper" (saltpeter) which was used in the past for pickling or preserving meat and sausages. The top sirloin cut is known as the "Bürgermeis-terstück" (means town mayor's cut) because, in the past, this fine gentleman was the only one who could afford to buy it!

Recipe by Brigitte Rückauf, Taunus

„Wersching" mit Meerrettichsoße und Kochfleisch

1 kg Suppenfleisch vom Rind (Brustkern)
1 Bd. Suppengrün
1 Prise Salz
1½ l Wasser

1 großer Kopf Wirsing (Wersching)
2 l Wasser
1 TL Salz
1 Msp. Natron
1 mittelgroße Zwiebel
100 g Dörrfleisch (durchwachsener, geräucherter Speck)
1½ EL Mehl
etwas Muskat nach Belieben

Soße

1 Stange (ca. 350 g) frischer Meerrettich
½ l Fleischbrühe
2 altbackene Brötchen, abgerieben
Salz
Pfeffer
Muskat nach Geschmack

Das Suppengrün putzen, waschen und klein schneiden. Das Fleisch kalt abwaschen und mit dem vorbereiteten Suppengrün in einen Topf geben. Mit Wasser auffüllen, sodass beides knapp bedeckt ist. Bei starker Hitze aufkochen lassen. Den Schaum auf der Oberfläche mit einer Schaumkelle immer wieder abschöpfen, damit die Fleischbrühe nicht trüb wird. Danach die Temperatur so weit reduzieren, dass die Brühe nur „leise köchelt" und der Topfdeckel halb geschlossen aufgelegt werden kann. Salz dazugeben und 1½–2 Stunden köcheln lassen.

Die Wirsingblätter ablösen, Wasser mit Salz und Natron zum Kochen bringen und den Wirsing darin 20–25 Minuten garen, bis die Blätter weich sind. Das Wasser abgießen und den Wirsing auf einem Sieb abtropfen lassen. Zwiebel schälen, Speck und Zwiebel in kleine Würfel schneiden und zusammen glasig braten. Mehl darüberstäuben, verrühren und anschwitzen. Das Mehl soll noch hell bleiben. Mit Wasser aufgießen, unter Rühren aufkochen, sodass eine leichte Bindung ohne Klümpchen entsteht.
Für die Soße die Meerrettichstange schälen und fein reiben. Fleischbrühe erhitzen. Brötchen in kleine Stücke schneiden, in die Fleischbrühe geben, auflösen, so dass eine Bindung entsteht. Meerrettich hinzufügen. Mit Salz und Pfeffer abschmecken, nach Belieben etwas Muskat darüberreiben.
Kurz vor dem Servieren das Fleisch aus der Brühe nehmen, etwas ruhen lassen und in dünnen Scheiben aufschneiden. Auf einer Platte anrichten und mit dem Wirsinggemüse, der Meerrettichsoße und Salzkartoffeln servieren.

Anmerkung

Bei diesem Gericht immer zuerst das Kochfleisch zubereiten, da ½ l Fleischbrühe für die Meerrettichsoße benötigt wird.
Wird nur der Wirsing mit Meerrettichsoße und Kartoffeln zubereitet, werden ¼ l der Wirsingbrühe und ¼ l Wasser verwendet. Für einen kräftigen Geschmack kann etwas mehr Dörrfleisch genommen werden.

Rezept von Hubert Schmidt, Taunus

Savoy Cabbage with Horseradish and Boiled Beef

2 lbs boiling beef (e.g. brisket)
1 bunch of soup greens
3 pts water

1 large Savoy cabbage
4 pts water
1 tsp salt
1 pinch of baking soda
1 medium sized onion
4 oz smoked streaky bacon
1½ tbsps flour
a little nutmeg to taste

Sauce

1 piece of fresh horseradish (approx. 12 oz)
1 pt meat stock (from the boiled beef)
2 stale bread rolls
salt
pepper
a little nutmeg to taste

Clean, wash and chop the greens. Rinse the meat under cold running water and place in a pan together with the prepared soup greens. Fill the pan with water so that it just covers the meat. Boil over a high heat.
Use a ladle to remove the foam from the surface of the water once in a while to prevent the meat stock from turning cloudy. Reduce the heat, so that the meat simmers gently and the lid can be left half open. Add the salt and simmer for a further 1½–2 hours.

Separate the leaves from the cabbage. Boil the water together with the salt and baking soda and cook the cabbage leaves for 20–25 minutes until they are soft. Pour off the water and leave the cabbage in a sieve to drain. Peel and dice the onion, then fry together with the diced bacon. Sprinkle with flour, stir and allow to sweat. Make sure the flour does not darken. Add the water and bring to the boil stirring constantly to form a light sauce with no lumps.

For the sauce

Peel and finely grate the fresh horseradish. Heat the meat stock. Cut the stale rolls into small pieces, add them to the stock and stir them into the liquid until it thickens. Add the horseradish. Season with salt and pepper, and add a little grated nutmeg to taste.
Just before serving, remove the meat from the stock. Leave it to stand for a moment and then cut into thin slices.
Serve the meat on a platter with the cabbage, horseradish sauce and boiled potatoes.

Comment

When preparing this meal, always begin with the boiled meat because 1 pint of meat stock is needed for the horseradish sauce.
If you only plan to serve the cabbage and horseradish sauce with potatoes, then use 1 cup of cabbage stock and 1 cup of water. For a stronger flavor, use a little more of the streaky bacon.

Recipe by Hubert Schmidt, Taunus

„Wersching" mit Meerrettichsoße und Kochfleisch
Savoy Cabbage with Horseradish and Boiled Beef

„Storzeniere" mit Hackfleischklößchen und Salzkartoffeln

1 kg frische Schwarzwurzeln (Storzeniere)
1 l Essigwasser
2 l Wasser
1 TL Salz
2 EL Milch

1 altbackenes Brötchen
1 Zwiebel
500 g gemischtes Hackfleisch
2 Eier
Salz
Pfeffer
3 EL Butter
250 g saure Sahne
3 EL Crème fraîche
Zitronensaft

500 g Kartoffeln, mehlig kochend
½ l Wasser
1 TL Salz

Schwarzwurzeln waschen und schälen, am besten mit Gummihandschuhen und unter Wasser. In Stücke schneiden und in Essigwasser legen, damit sie nicht schwarz werden. Wasser mit Salz und Milch zum Kochen bringen und die „Storzeniere" darin 10–15 Minuten vorgaren, heraus nehmen. Kochflüssigkeit zur Seite stellen und aufbewahren.

Brötchen in warmem Wasser einweichen. Die Zwiebel schälen und in feine Würfel schneiden. Brötchen ausdrücken, mit Hackfleisch, Eiern, Zwiebelwürfeln, Salz und Pfeffer gut vermengen. Den Hackfleischteig zu Klößchen von ca. 4 cm Durchmesser formen. Butter heiß werden lassen. Die Schwarzwurzeln und 400 ml der „Storzeniere"-Kochflüssigkeit dazugeben. Die Hackklößchen einlegen und 10 Minuten bei starker Hitze kochen lassen. Wärmezufuhr reduzieren und weitere 5 Minuten ziehen lassen. Saure Sahne und Crème fraîche unterrühren, mit Salz, Pfeffer und einem kleinen Schuss Zitronensaft abschmecken. Kartoffeln schälen und in gleich große Stücke schneiden. Kartoffeln in Salzwasser kalt aufsetzen, zum Kochen bringen und in ca. 20 Minuten gar kochen. Von den Kartoffeln das Wasser abschütten, den Topf nochmals ganz kurz auf die Herdplatte stellen und die Kartoffeln im offenen Topf abdampfen lassen, damit sie schön trocken werden und die Soße gut aufnehmen können.

Anmerkung

Der mundartliche Begriff „Storzeniere" stammt vermutlich vom Lateinischen ab und gründet auf einer hessischen Verballhornung von Scorzonera, einer Pflanzengattung, zu der die Schwarzwurzel gehört.

Rezept von Helga Bachmann, Nordhessen

Salsify with meatballs and boiled potatoes

2 lbs fresh salsify
2 pts vinegar water
4 pts water
1 tsp salt
2 tbsps milk

1 stale bread roll
1 onion
1 lb mixed ground mince (beef & pork)
2 eggs
salt
pepper
3 tbsp butter
8 fl oz sour cream
3 tbsps crème fraîche
lemon juice

1 lb potatoes (floury)
1 pt water
1 tsp salt

Wash and peel the salsify under running water –
it is best to do this wearing rubber gloves.
Cut into pieces and place in the vinegar water to
prevent them from turning black. Bring the water,
salt and milk to the boil and blanch the salsify for
10 to 15 minutes. Remove the salsify from the
water and keep the liquid for later.

Soak the rolls in warm water. Peel and finely dice
the onion. Squeeze out the bread rolls and mix
well with the ground mince, eggs, onion, salt and
pepper. Form the mixture to meat balls about
1½ inches in diameter. Heat the butter. Add the
salsify and about 2 cups of the salsify stock. Place
the meatballs in the liquid and boil vigorously for
10 minutes. Reduce the heat and leave to simmer
for a further 5 minutes. Stir in the sour cream and
the crème fraiche. Season with salt, pepper and a
dash of lemon juice.
Peel the potatoes and cut into similar sized
chunks. Place them in a pan of cold salt water,
bring to the boil and cook for approximately
20 minutes. Drain off the water and return the
potatoes to the heat for a moment, without the
lid on, to cook off any excess water so that they
are nice and dry and can absorb the sauce well.

Comment

The local term "Storzeniere" is probably a Hessian
adaptation of the Latin word "Scorzonera", a type
of plant in the sub-family of the Cichorioideae, of
which salsify is a member.

Recipe by Helga Bachmann, Nordhessen

Wetzstahkließ mit Specksoße
Dumplings with Bacon Sauce

Wetzstahkließ mit Specksoße

4 Portionen

  1 kg große gelbe Kartoffeln, festkochend
  ¾ l Milch
je 1 Prise Salz, Pfeffer, Muskat
175 g Grieß
  2 l Wasser, 1 EL Salz
200 g Dörrfleisch (durchwachsener
    Räucherspeck)
  1 große Zwiebel, 1 TL Mehl
  ½ l Milch oder Wasser

Kartoffeln fein reiben, sofort in ein Leinentuch geben, damit sie nicht braun werden. Die Kartoffelmasse sehr gut ausdrücken, sodass der Kloßteig ganz trocken ist. Milch mit den Gewürzen erwärmen, Grieß darin zu einem festen Brei kochen. Heiß zu dem Kartoffelteig geben, gut durchkneten und nochmals abschmecken. Mit den Händen aus der Masse längliche, 6–7 cm lange Klößchen rollen. Wasser zum Kochen bringen, Salz zufügen, Klößchen einlegen und die Hitze reduzieren, sodass das Wasser nur noch leicht siedet. Im offenen Topf ca. 25 Minuten garen. Die Klöße mehrmals mit einem Kochlöffel im Wasser umwälzen, damit sie nicht an der Oberfläche austrocknen.
Für die Soße Speck in kleine Würfel schneiden und anbraten. Zwiebel in Würfel schneiden und mitbraten, bis sie glasig sind. Mehl darüberstäuben, verrühren und anschwitzen, ohne dass das Mehl braun wird. Mit Milch oder Wasser ablöschen und dabei gut umrühren. Ca. 10 Minuten kochen lassen, dabei immer wieder rühren.

Anmerkung

Die Form der Klößchen erinnert an einen Wetzstein, mit dem man z. B. Sensen schärfte. So ist der Name entstanden.
Hessische Frage: Wie viel Kließ kammer off aa mol esse? 5! – 1 im Mund, 1 uff de Gawwel, 1 uffm Deller, 2 im Auge.

Rezept von Brigitte Rückauf, Taunus

Salzekuchen

8–10 Portionen

225 g Speck
625 g Zwiebeln
  ¼ l Sonnenblumenöl
750 g heiße Kartoffeln, gekocht
    (Kloßkartoffeln)
  1/8 l Milch
375 g Quark (Magerstufe), 2 Eier
  ¼ l saure Sahne oder Schmand
  1 Bd. Petersilie, gehackt
etwas Salz
750 g Roggenbrotteig mit Natursauerteig
    (vom Bäcker, vorher bestellen)
etwas Fett für das Kuchenblech

Backofen auf 240 °C vorheizen. Speck in kleine Würfel schneiden und in einer Pfanne auslassen, Sonnenblumenöl dazugeben. Die Zwiebeln in feine Würfel schneiden und mit dem Speck glasig dünsten. Die Kartoffeln durch eine Kartoffelpresse drücken und mit der heißen Milch in einer großen Schüssel zu Brei verarbeiten. Quark, Eier, saure Sahne, Speck mit Öl und Zwiebeln sowie die Petersilie zum Kartoffelbrei geben, gut verrühren und mit Salz abschmecken.
Den Brotteig auf einem Kuchenblech auswellen und die Kartoffelmasse gleichmäßig darauf verstreichen, am Rand etwas freilassen und den Brotteig nach innen umlegen. Im Backofen ca. 30 Minuten backen.

Anmerkung

Diese Zubereitung stammt aus dem Vogelsberg und der „Salzekuche" wird dort häufig in restaurierten Brotbacköfen gebacken. Die Menge reicht aus für ein großes, rundes Blech mit einem Durchmesser von 70 cm. Das entspricht etwa zwei haushaltsüblichen Backofenblechen.
Ein Rezept, wie gemacht für große Feiern, auch in kleineren Stückchen als Fingerfood zu essen.

Rezept von Hilde Gromes, Vogelsberg

Dumplings with Bacon Sauce

2 lbs large yellow waxy potatoes
3 cups milk
a pinch of salt, pepper and grated nutmeg
6 oz semolina, 4 pts water
1 tbsp salt
7 oz streaky smoked bacon
1 large onion
1 tsp flour
1 pt milk or water

Finely grate the potatoes then wrap them in a clean cloth to prevent them from turning brown. Squeeze out any liquid from the potatoes so that they are completely dry. Warm the milk with the spices, add the semolina and then cook until stiff. While still hot, mix the semolina and the grated potato, knead well and then season to taste. Using your hands, form dumplings that are about 2½ inches long. Bring the water to the boil, then add the salt, and put the dumplings in the pan. Reduce the heat, so that the water is barely simmering and cook for approx. 25 minutes. With a wooden spoon, turn the dumplings several times to prevent them from drying out on top.
For the sauce, dice and fry the bacon. Add the diced onions to the pan, and fry until them until they are glazed. Sprinkle with flour, stir, taking care that the flour does not turn brown. Add the milk or water and stir well. Allow to cook for approx. 10 minutes, stirring from time to time.

Comment

The shape of the dumplings is like a whetstone for sharpening tools e. g. scythes, and this is where they get their name "Wetzstahkließ".

Old Hessian saying

How many dumplings can you eat in one go? 5! One in your mouth, one on your fork, one on your plate and two in your eyes!

Recipe by Brigitte Rückauf, Taunus

Salty Cake

8–10 servings

  8 oz smoked streaky bacon
1¼ lbs onions
  1 cup sunflower oil
1½ lbs hot cooked boiled potatoes
    (floury potatoes)
  1 cup milk
13 oz low fat curd cheese
  2 eggs
  1 cup sour cream or heavy sour cream
  1 bunch of parsley (chopped)
a little salt
1¾ lbs natural sour dough (from your baker, you may need to pre-order)
a little butter for the baking tray

Pre-heat the oven to 460 °F. Dice the bacon into small cubes and heat in a frying pan to melt off the fat. Add the sunflower oil and fry the finely diced onions with the bacon until they are glazed. Mash the potatoes in a bowl together with the hot milk. Add the curd cheese, eggs, sour cream, bacon, oil, onions and parsley to the mashed potatoes, stir well and season with salt.
Roll out the sour dough on the baking tray and spread with the potato mixture, leaving the edges free. Fold over the edges of the dough to form a ridge, so that the topping doesn't leak, and bake in the oven for approx. 30 minutes.

Comment

This recipe comes from Vogelsberg and is often baked in restored village baking ovens. The recipe is enough for one round baking tray from a village baking oven with a diameter of about 27½ inches. That's the equivalent of 2 standard sized domestic baking trays 18 × 14 inches in size.
An ideal recipe for large celebrations. Just cut into small pieces and serve as finger food.

Recipe by Hilde Gromes, Vogelsberg

Woihinkelche

2 Hähnchen (à 1200 g)
3 Knoblauchzehen
Salz
30 g Fett (Bratöl oder Butterschmalz)
2 EL Weinbrand, 2 Zwiebeln
400 g frische Champignons
½ l trockener Weißwein (Riesling)
1 Zweiglein Estragon
⅛ l Sahne, 4 Eigelbe
Petersilie, Pfeffer

Hähnchen in zwei Teile zerschneiden und die Schenkel abtrennen. Von den restlichen Teilen das Fleisch auslösen. Knoblauch schälen, durch eine Knoblauchpresse drücken und mit Salz vermischen. Alle Hähnchenteile damit einreiben und dann im heißen Fett anbraten. Mit Weinbrand übergießen und flambieren. Aus der Pfanne nehmen. Zwiebeln schälen, in Würfel schneiden. Champignons putzen und in Viertel schneiden. Im Bratfett andünsten und mit Wein ablöschen. Die Hähnchenteile wieder zufügen und Estragon hineingeben. Zugedeckt 20–30 Minuten garen. Eigelbe mit Sahne verrühren, Petersilie hacken. Hähnchenfleisch von der Kochstelle nehmen, Estragon entfernen und die Eier-Sahne in die nicht mehr kochende Flüssigkeit rühren. Alles heiß werden lassen, aber nicht mehr kochen. Mit Salz und Pfeffer abschmecken. Mit Petersilie bestreuen und mit Salzkartoffeln servieren.

Anmerkung

Die Hähnchenschenkel werden mit dem Knochen geschmort, weil sie dadurch mehr Geschmack geben. Außerdem lässt sich das Fleisch dann besser vom Knochen lösen.
Je nach Vorliebe mehr Estragon verwenden.
Ein Rheingau-Riesling passt für dieses Gericht natürlich am allerbesten!

Rezept von Kai Uwe Korn, Eltville

Weckewerk

250 g altbackenes Weißbrot oder Brötchen
1 l Bouillon (Rezept S. 80)
250 g Zwiebeln
750 g Schlachtfleischreste vom Schwein mit
    Schwarte, gegart; alternativ:
    Schweinehackfleisch und eine Schwarte
1 TL Kümmel
1 TL Majoran, getrocknet
Salz
Pfeffer

Brot in der heißen Fleischbrühe in einem großen Topf quellen lassen. Zwiebel schälen und in große Stücke schneiden. Fleisch, Schwarte und Zwiebeln durch den Fleischwolf drehen. Alles in die Bouillon geben, mit Kümmel, Majoran, Salz und Pfeffer abschmecken und unter ständigem Rühren zu einer festen Masse verkochen.
Entweder frisch zubereitet mit einer sauren Gurke zu Pellkartoffeln reichen oder im Kühlschrank erkalten lassen.
Zum Servieren Scheiben von der Masse abschneiden und in der Pfanne braten. Dazu passen auch Pellkartoffeln und saure Gurken.

Anmerkung

In Nordhessen kann man die Weckewerkmasse beim Metzger vorbereitet kaufen.
Eine Mahlzeit, die ein kühles Bier und einen Schnaps verträgt!

Hessischer Humor ist durchaus eigen:

Fragt eine Kundin: „Sin die Schweinsfüssjer aach werklich frisch?"
Sagt die Metzgersfrau: „Wann Se die kitzele, hör'n Se die Sau noch lache!"

Rezept von Susanne Lengemann-Kampe, Kassel

Hessian Coq au Vin

2 chickens (each 2½ lbs in weight)
3 cloves of garlic
salt
1 oz clarified butter or frying oil
2 tbsps brandy
2 onions
14 oz fresh mushrooms
1 pt dry white wine (Riesling)
4 egg yolks, 1 sprig of tarragon
½ cup cream
parsley, pepper

Cut the chickens in half and remove the legs.
De-bone the rest of the chicken.
Peel and crush the garlic, then mix it with the salt.
Rub the chicken pieces with the garlic paste.
Heat the oil and brown the chicken pieces. Add
the brandy and flambé the chicken. Remove from
the pan.
Peel and dice the onions then clean and quarter
the mushrooms. Fry them in the same pan that was
used for the chicken. Add the cooked chicken
pieces and tarragon. Cover and leave to cook for
20–30 minutes. Mix the egg yolk with the cream.
Chop the parsley. Remove the chicken from the
heat, take out the tarragon and stir in the eggs
and cream once the juices have cooled a little and
are no longer boiling. Reheat, but do not allow to
boil.
Season with salt and pepper. Serve with boiled
potatoes.

Comment

The chicken thighs are cooked on the bone
because they retain their flavor better that way.
The meat is also easier to remove from the bone
once the legs are cooked.
More tarragon can be used according to taste.
A Rheingau-Riesling white wine is of course the
best wine for this recipe!

Recipe by Kai Uwe Korn, Eltville

Pork Sausagemeat

8 oz stale white bread or rolls.
2 pts meat stock (page 81)
4 oz onions
1¾ lbs poached pork scraps with rinds
alternative: pork mince and a piece of pork
    rind.
1 tsp caraway
1 tsp marjoram
salt
pepper

Leave the bread and meat stock to soak in a large
pan. Peel and cut the onions into large chunks.
Run the meat, rind and onions through a meat
grinder. Put everything into the stock together
with the caraway and marjoram, salt and pepper
and then boil the mixture stirring constantly until
the mixture becomes stiff.
Serve straight away with a pickled cucumber and
boiled potatoes or chill in the fridge.
To serve later, cut a slice of the mixture and shallow
fry. Serve as above with pickled cucumber and
boiled potatoes.

Note

In the north of Hesse "Weckewerk" mixture can
be bought ready to cook at the local butchers.
A meal which is perfect served with a cool beer or
a schnapps!

Humor in Hesse is very distinctive.
Here is a typical joke:

At the butcher's store, a customer asks the
woman behind the counter, "Are the pig's
trotters really fresh?"
The woman answers: "Well, if you tickle
them you can still hear the pig laugh!"

Repice by Susanne Lengemann-Kampe, Kassel

Taunusforelle Müllerin-Art mit Petersilienkartoffeln und Kopfsalat

4 frische Forellen (à ca. 350 g)
50 g Mehl
Salz
Pfeffer
½ Bd. Petersilie
4 Zweiglein Dill oder 4 Blatt Bärlauch
oder 25 g Kräuterbutter
(anstelle der frischen Kräuter)
20 g Butter
100 ml Rapsöl

Kopfsalat

1 Kopfsalat
2 EL Sonnenblumenöl
2 EL Schmand
1 Msp. mittelscharfer Senf
1 EL Essig
Salz
Pfeffer
½ Bd. krause Petersilie
½ Bd. Schnittlauch

Forellen ausnehmen und unter kaltem Wasser abspülen, die schleimige Schicht auf der Haut belassen und nicht verletzen. Außen und innen salzen und pfeffern. Mehl auf einen großen Teller sieben, die Forellen darin wenden und mit den Kräutern füllen. Öl erhitzen, Forellen von jeder Seite 5–6 Minuten darin braten. Kurz vor Ende der Garzeit Butter hinzufügen, Forellen fertig braten und währenddessen immer wieder mit der Ölbutter begießen.

Petersilienkartoffeln

1 kg kleine Kartoffeln, festkochend
2 l Wasser
1 TL Salz
80 g Butter
1 Bd. krause Petersilie

Kartoffeln waschen, schälen, im Salzwasser 20 Minuten gar kochen, abschütten. Petersilie putzen, waschen, fein hacken. Butter zu den heißen Kartoffeln geben, ebenso die gehackte Petersilie. Deckel auflegen und die Kartoffeln im Topf gut schwenken.

Vom Salat die einzelnen Blätter ablösen, waschen, in mundgerechte Stückchen zupfen, gut abtrocknen lassen oder trocken schleudern. Für die Salatsoße alle Zutaten miteinander verrühren. Kräuter putzen, waschen, klein schneiden und zufügen. Alles gut verrühren, abschmecken. Kurz vor dem Servieren den Salat mit der Soße anmachen.

Tipps

Die Butter erst gegen Ende der Bratzeit zu den Forellen geben, damit sie nicht schwarz wird. Durch Begießen mit der Ölbutter bekommen die Fische einen zarten Buttergeschmack, trocknen nicht aus und werden auf beiden Seiten schön knusprig.

Anmerkung

Frisch gefangene Taunusforellen werden in Hessen von Anglern oft selbst in eigenen kleinen Räucheröfen geräuchert und am liebsten noch warm verzehrt. Mit etwas Sahnemeerrettich und einer frischen, knusprigen Scheibe Roggenmischbrot ist dies eine echte Delikatesse und als Vorspeise beliebt.

Rezept von Beate Plohmer, Taunus

Taunus trout à la Meunière with Parsley Potatoes and Lettuce

4 fresh trout
  (each approx. 12 oz in weight)
2 oz flour
salt
pepper
  ½ bunch of parsley
  4 sprigs of dill or 4 leaves of wild garlic
  (ramson)
or 1 oz herb butter
  (instead of the fresh herbs)
  2 oz flour
  1 oz butter
  ½ cup rapeseed oil

Gut the trout and rinse under cold water. Take care not to damage the layer of mucus covering the skin of the fish. Sprinkle the inside and outside of the trout with salt and pepper. Sieve the flour onto a large plate, roll the trout in the flour and fill the fish with herbs.
Heat the oil and fry the fish on both sides for 5–6 minutes. Just before the fish has finished cooking, add the butter to the pan. Finish frying the trout, spooning over the melted butter mixed with oil as the fish cooks.

Parsley potatoes

2 lbs small potatoes (waxy)
4 pts water
1 tsp salt
3 oz butter
1 bunch of curled parsley

Wash and peel the potatoes. Cook them for 20 minutes until done, and then drain. Clean, wash and finely chop the parsley. Add the butter and parsley to the hot potatoes, then replace the lid of the saucepan and toss them in the herb butter.

Recipe by Beate Plohmer, Taunus

Lettuce

1 lettuce
2 tbsps sunflower oil
2 tbsps heavy sour cream
a little medium hot mustard
1 tbsp vinegar
salt
pepper
½ bunch of curled parsley
½ bunch of chives

Separate the lettuce leaves, then wash and tear into bite-sized pieces. Dry well with a clean tea towel or a salad spinner. For the dressing, mix all the remaining ingredients together. Clean, wash and finely chop the herbs. Mix everything together well and season. Just before serving pour on the dressing.

Tips

Don't add the butter to the trout until it is nearly cooked – otherwise it will turn black.
Spooning the oil and melted butter over the fish gives them a buttery taste and a crunchy skin on both sides and prevents them from drying out.

Comment

Freshly caught Taunus trout is best enjoyed warm, just as the anglers enjoy it who eat it fresh from the small smoking ovens that they use to smoke their catch.
Served with a little horseradish cream and a fresh slice of rye bread, this Hessian delicacy is a popular starter.

Zanderfilet nach Frankfurter-Art
Pike-perch, Frankfurt Style

Zanderfilet
nach Frankfurter-Art

1 kg Zanderfilet
30 g Butter
½ Zitrone (Saft)
Salz
Pfeffer
1 Zwiebel
1 Salatgurke
250 m Sahne
1 Bd. Dill

Anmerkung

Die Frankfurter Küche besaß ab dem 16. Jahrhundert einen guten Ruf. Gasthöfe in Frankfurt waren bis weit in den europäischen Raum berühmt für ihre Köstlichkeiten. Zander aus den heimischen Gewässern wurde einst vorrangig in der bürgerlichen Küche und dort auf vielfältige Art zubereitet.

Backofen auf 180 °C vorheizen. Fisch säubern und trocken tupfen. Eine feuerfeste Form mit etwas Butter ausstreichen. Den Fisch hineinlegen und mit Zitronensaft beträufeln. Salz und Pfeffer darüber streuen. Zwiebel in feine Würfel schneiden und auf dem Fisch verteilen. Im Backofen zugedeckt ca. 30 Minuten dünsten.
Salatgurke mit der Schale in 1 cm dicke Scheiben schneiden, Salz und Pfeffer darüberstreuen. Sahne zum Kochen bringen und die Gurken darin 15 Minuten bei geringer Wärmezufuhr köcheln lassen. Salatgurken mit einer Schaumkelle herausnehmen, gut abtropfen lassen. Auf eine Platte geben und die Fischfilets darauf anrichten. Den Fischsud zur Sahne geben und einkochen, bis die Soße dicklich wird. Dill putzen, waschen, Spitzen abzupfen und klein schneiden. In die Soße geben und abschmecken. Soße über den Fisch gießen, mit Salzkartoffeln und einem frischen Salat servieren.

Rezept von Herbert Hettler, Frankfurt

Pike-perch, Frankfurt Style

2 lbs pike-perch
1½ oz butter
juice of ½ a lemon
salt
pepper
  1 onion
  1 cucumber
  1 cup cream
  1 bunch of dill

Pre-heat the oven to 350°F. Clean the fish and pat it dry. Butter a flameproof dish and place the fish in it. Squeeze the lemon juice over the fish and sprinkle with salt and pepper. Cover and steam in the oven for approx. 30 minutes.
Cut the cucumber into slices about half an inch thick then sprinkle the slices with salt and pepper. Boil the cream and simmer the cucumber slices in it for 15 minutes over a low heat. Remove the cucumber slices with a ladle and drain well. Arrange them on serving platter and place the fish fillets on top.
Add the fish stock to the cream and reduce until you have a thick sauce. Clean and wash the dill. Remove the tips from the dill sprigs and chop finely. Add to the sauce and season to taste. Pour the sauce over the fish and serve with fresh salad and boiled potatoes.

Comment
Frankfurt's cuisine has a good reputation that dates back to the 16th century, when its inns were famous throughout Europe for their delicacies. In the past, local pike-perch was extremely popular and was prepared in many different ways by the middle classes.

Recipe by Herbert Hettler, Frankfurt

Grie Sooß mit gekochten Eiern und Kartoffeln
Green Sauce with boiled Eggs and Potatoes

Grie Sooß

Mayonnaise

1 Eigelb (zimmerwarm)
½ Teelöffel Essig
150–200 ml Pflanzenöl
½ TL Senf
Salz
Pfeffer
1 TL Zitronensaft

Alle Zutaten müssen zimmerwarm temperiert sein, damit die Mayonnaise gelingt.
Eigelb und Essig (Essig hilft beim Gelingen der Mayonnaise) mit einer Gabel oder einem Handrührgerät in einer Schale gründlich aufschlagen, bis das Eigelb heller geworden ist.
Öl in kleinen Tropfen, später in einem sehr dünnen Strahl, unter Rühren zum Eigelb gießen. Erst weiteres Öl zufügen, wenn die vorherige Menge vollständig untergeschlagen ist. Nach und nach wird die Masse heller und dicker, bis die Mayonnaise steif ist. Sie löst sich dann etwas von der Schalenwand und bleibt an der Gabel hängen. Mit Senf, Salz, Pfeffer und Zitronensaft würzen.

Grie Sooß

50 g Mayonnaise
¼ l saure Sahne
1 Zitrone (Saft)
3–4 Eier, hart gekocht
Salz, Pfeffer, Zucker
7 verschiedene* Kräuter,
insgesamt ca. 200 g: Schnittlauch, Sauerampfer, Petersilie, Gartenkresse, Borretsch, Kerbel, Pimpernell

Mayonnaise mit saurer Sahne und Zitronensaft verrühren. Eier pellen, fein hacken und zufügen. Mit Salz, Pfeffer und Zucker abschmecken. Kräuter verlesen, waschen, gut trocknen, sehr fein wiegen und zur Soße geben.

Anmerkung

Ein schnelles, gesundes Gericht ist die Grie Sooß mit hart gekochten Eiern. Pro Portion werden 2 Eier mit der Soße und Salzkartoffeln gereicht. Bekannt, geliebt und wunderbar ist die Kombination mit Rindfleisch und Kartoffeln (Seite 28).
Es existieren viele Varianten der grünen Soße. Jeder schwört auf sein eigenes Rezept, verteidigt es vehement und behauptet, es sei das einzig „echte"!

Originalrezept, Rhein-Main-Gebiet

Nordhessische Version

3 EL Öl
½ TL Kräuteressig
1 TL Senf
Salz, Pfeffer
etwas Zucker
250 g Magerquark
1 Becher saure Sahne oder Joghurt (200 g)
2 Becher Schmand (à 200 g)
200 g Kräuter: Petersilie, Dill, Pimpernell, Sauerampfer, Borretsch
1–2 Frühlingszwiebeln (Schlotten)

Öl, Essig, Senf, Salz, Pfeffer und Zucker mit der Gabel sämig aufschlagen. Dann Quark, Sahne sowie Kräuter und „Schlotten", jeweils gewaschen, abgetrocknet und fein gewogen, dazugeben.
Zum Schluss pro Person (!) 2–3 hart gekochte, gehackte Eier und, falls die Soße zu dick ist, etwas Milch dazugießen.

---

* Gemischt je nach Jahreszeit und was der Kräutergarten bietet; wichtig ist, dass es diese 7 Sorten sind!

Rezept von Monika Trost, Waldeck

Green Sauce

Mayonnaise

 1 egg yolk (room temperature)
 ½ tsp vinegar
approx. 5 fl oz vegetable oil (a little more
      if needed)
 ½ tbsp mustard
salt, pepper
 1 tsp lemon juice

For the mayonnaise to work, all ingredients must
be at room temperature.
Beat the egg yolk and vinegar with a fork (or hand
mixer) in a bowl until the egg yolk turns pale in
color. Slowly pour in the oil, drop by drop to begin
with, beating all the time. Only add more oil once
the rest has been thoroughly incorporated into
the mixture. Bit by bit, the mixture will thicken
until the mayonnaise is stiff, at which point the
mixture will come off the sides of the bowl and
stick to the fork.
Season with salt, pepper and lemon juice.

Comment

The vinegar helps make a successful mayonnaise

Green Sauce

 ¼ cup mayonnaise
 1 cup sour cream
 1 lemon (juice)
3–4 eggs, hard boiled
salt, pepper, sugar
approx. 8 oz of 7 different* herbs:
      chives, sorrel, parsley, garden cress, chervil
      borage, pimpernel

Mix the mayonnaise with the sour cream and
lemon juice. Peel and finely chop the eggs, then
add them to the mixture. Season to taste with
salt, pepper and sugar. Sort, wash and dry the
herbs well. Chop them very finely before adding
them to the sauce.

Comment

Green Sauce with Hard Boiled Eggs is a
quick and healthy meal. For each serving you will
need 2 eggs, boiled potatoes and the sauce.
This tastes wonderful and is very popular *served
with Boiled Beef and Potatoes* (page 29)
There are many variations of Green Sauce and
everyone swears by their own recipe, vehemently
claiming it to be the only "real" version!

This recipe is originally from Rhein-Main area.

Variation from North Hesse

 3 tbsps oil
 ½ tsp herb vinegar
 1 tsp mustard
salt, pepper
a little sugar
 1 cup of low fat curd cheese
 1 pot of sour cream or yogurt
      (approx. 7 fl oz)
 2 pots of heavy sour cream (13½ fl oz)

Beat the oil, herb vinegar, mustard, salt and
pepper, and the sugar with a fork until you have
a creamy vinaigrette sauce, then add the low
fat curd cheese, cream, heavy sour cream, parsley,
dill, scallions, pimpernel, sorrel, borage, and
chives. Finally, add 2–3 chopped hard boiled eggs
per person. If the mixture seems too thick, add
a little milk.

---

*   Always use a mix of these 7 herbs, in equal amounts as far as
    the season allows!

Recipe by Monika Trost, Waldeck

Rippche mit Kraut
Pork Loin with Cabbage

Rippche mit Kraut

800–1000 g gepökelte Kammrippchen am
    Stück (durchwachsen und saftig)
etwas Salz
    2 Zwiebeln, gespickt mit 2 Nelken und
      Lorbeerblättern
    1 Bd. Suppengrün
    50 g Schweineschmalz, 1 kg rohes Sauerkraut
150 g durchwachsener Speck
Zucker nach Geschmack
    8 Wachholderbeeren, 6 Pfefferkörner
    2 Lorbeerblätter, ½ TL Kümmel
    ¼ l Bouillon (Rezept S. 80)
    ¼ l Wasser

Rippchen in einem Topf mit kaltem Wasser auffüllen, sodass das Fleisch mit Wasser knapp bedeckt ist. Zwiebeln mit Lorbeerblättern und Nelken spicken. Suppengrün putzen, waschen, kleinschneiden und mit der gespickten Zwiebel zum Fleisch geben. 2 Stunden bei ca. 80 °C sieden lassen. Das Wasser sollte nicht kochen. Schmalz in einen Topf geben. Sauerkraut etwas auseinanderzupfen und mit dem ganzen Stück Speck kurze Zeit durchschmoren. Zucker und Gewürze (in ein Mullsäckchen gebunden) hinzugeben, gut umrühren und mit Bouillon und Wasser angießen. Das Kraut ca. 30 Minuten dünsten. Dabei immer wieder umrühren, verkochte Flüssigkeit mit Wasser ergänzen. Gegarte Rippchen entlang der Knochen in Scheiben schneiden und mit dem Kraut anrichten. Der Hesse mag's mit Kartoffelbrei oder frischem Roggenbrot. Mittelscharfer Senf passt gut dazu.

Anmerkung

Fettärmer sind gepökelte Stielrippchen (die mageren Kotelettstücke vom Schwein). Werden die Rippchen am Vortag gegart, werden sie im Krautbett langsam erwärmt; nicht kochen, sonst werden sie trocken.

Rezept von Lotti Henrici, Taunus

Handkäs

    2 l nicht homogenisierte Milch
10 g Salz
    2 g Speisenatron (Backsoda)
etwas Kümmel

Nicht homogenisierte Milch ca. 10 Stunden bei 10–12 °C stehen lassen. Während dieser Zeit bildet sich auf der Oberfläche Rahm, diesen dann mit einem Löffel abheben. Er lässt sich sehr gut für Soßen oder Süßspeisen verwenden.
Die entrahmte Milch etwa 2 Tage bei Raumtemperatur stehen lassen, dann in ein Leinentuch oder eine Stoffwindel geben und die Molke herauspressen, die Molke zur späteren Behandlung der Handkäse im Kühlschrank aufbewahren.
Das Tuch an den vier Enden zusammenbinden und aufhängen. Unter das Tuch unbedingt eine Schüssel stellen, in die in den nächsten 24 Stunden die restliche Molke abfließen kann.
Nun die Masse (auch Matte genannt) mit ca. 5 % Speisesalz und 1 % Natron mischen und verkneten. Von Hand kleine Käselaibe formen und auf einen Rost (z. B. aus dem Backofen) setzen. Mit einem Tuch bedeckt bei 12–16 °C gut 14 Tage reifen lassen. Die Handkäse sollten jeden Tag mit Molke und Essigwasser abgewaschen werden.
Danach können die Handkäse, je nach Geschmack mit Kümmel bestreut, in Wachspapier gewickelt im Kühlschrank gelagert werden.
Serviert wird der Handkäs mit „Musik" (Zutaten siehe Seite 58).

Anmerkung

Das ist nur eines von 250 Rezepten aus der Sammlung von Manfred Seuss zur Handkäs-Herstellung!

Rezept von Manfred Seuss, Taunus

Pork Loin with Cabbage

1 piece of cured pork loin rib 1¾–2 lbs
   weight (marbled and juicy)
a little salt
2 onions, 2 cloves, bay leaves
1 bunch of soup greens
1½ oz pork dripping
2 lbs raw pickled cabbage
5 oz streaky smoked bacon, sugar to taste
8 juniper berries, 6 pepper corns
2 bay leaves, ½ tsp caraway
1 cup meat stock (page 81), 1 cup water

Place the pork loin in a pan and fill with cold water until barely covered.

Lard the onion with the bay leaves and cloves. Clean and finely cut the soup greens. Place them in the pan together with the meat and the larded onion. Simmer for 2 hours at approx 175°F. Do not allow to boil.

Heat the dripping in a pan. Pull the pickled cabbage apart a little and leave it to stew for a while together with the whole piece of bacon. Put the sugar and the spices in a small muslin bag and add them to the pan. Stir well and pour in the meat stock and the water.

Stew the cabbage for about 30 minutes, stirring occasionally, replacing any evaporated liquid with water.

Cut the cooked loin into chops along the bone. Serve the chops with the cabbage.

In Hesse people like to serve this with mashed potatoes or fresh rye bread. It's also good with medium hot mustard.

Comment

If you don't like fatty food, then you can use boneless pork loin.

If the chops are cooked the day before, they should be placed between layers of cabbage and warmed slowly until warm. Don't boil them or they will dry out.

Recipe by Lotti Henrici, Taunus

Handcheese

4 pts non-homogenized milk
¾ tbsp salt
½ tsp baking soda from the pharmacy
some caraway seeds

Leave the non-homogenized milk to stand for about 10 hours at about 50°F. After a while, cream will collect on the surface of the milk. Remove this with a spoon (it's ideal for sauces or desserts).

Leave the milk to stand for a further 2 days at room temperature, then place it in a linen cloth and squeeze out the whey.

Keep the whey in the fridge for later.

Tie the four corners of the cloth together and hang it up over a bowl so that the remaining whey can drip into it for another 24 hrs.

Now mix the curds with 5% salt and 1% baking powder. Knead the mixture well, and then shape it into small cheeses with your hands. Place the cheeses on a wire rack (e. g. from the oven). Cover with a clean cloth and leave to ripen for 12–14 days.

Wash the hand cheeses every day with the whey and vinegar-water.

After 14 days, the cheeses can be sprinkled with caraway seed and stored in the fridge wrapped in wax paper.

Comment

This is only one of 250 recipes for handcheese that have been collected by Mr Seuss!

Recipe by Manfred Seuss, Taunus

Handkäs mit „Musik"
Handcheese with "Music"

Kochkäs oder Brennkäs mit „Musik"

4–5 Portionen
 1 kg Schichtkäse
 3 TL Natron
30 g Butter
50 ml Sahne
 1 Eigelb
etwas Salz

„Musik"
 1 Zwiebel
 6 EL Weißweinessig
 4 EL Sonnenblumenöl
 4 EL Wasser
schwarzer Pfeffer

Garnitur
je 1 TL Schnittlauch und Petersilie, fein gehackt
Salz

Den Schichtkäse in ein Leinentuch einschlagen und in ein Sieb legen. Den Käse beschweren und einige Stunden abtropfen lassen. Den Schichtkäse in eine feuerfeste Schüssel geben, Natron gut mit dem Käse vermischen. 2–3 Stunden stehen lassen. Der Käse muss zerlaufen.
In einem Kochtopf Wasser erhitzen und die Schüssel mit dem Käse in das Wasserbad hängen. Unter ständigem Rühren erhitzen (Der Käse darf nicht über 70 °C heiß werden!). Sobald eine cremige Masse ohne Klumpen entstanden ist, den Käse aus dem Wasserbad nehmen, Butter, Sahne und Eigelb unterrühren und mit Salz abschmecken. Abkühlen lassen.
Für die Zwiebelsoße – die hessische „Musik" – die Zwiebel fein hacken, mit Essig, Öl, Wasser und Pfeffer würzen, gut verrühren. Kochkäse auf Teller verteilen, die Zwiebelsoße darübergeben, mit den Gartenkräutern bestreuen und nach Geschmack salzen.

Rezept von Mathias Fleischmann, Odenwald

Anmerkung
Traditionell wird Kochkäse auf einem kräftigen Bauernbrot, dick mit Butter bestrichen, gegessen und, wer's mag, streut Kümmel darauf.
Im Odenwald wird Kochkäse als „exotische" Beigabe zu Bratwurst oder als sogenanntes Kochkäseschnitzel angeboten: ein Wiener Schnitzel, frisch aus der Pfanne, auf dem sich der Kochkäse lecker anschmiegt. Wichtig: den Teller dazu erwärmen!

Cooked Cheese with "Music"

4–5 servings

2 lbs baking cheese
3 tsp baking soda
1 oz butter
3½ tbsp cream
1 egg yolk
a little salt

Hessian "Music"

1 onion
6 tbsps white wine vinegar
4 tbsps sunflower oil
4 tbsps water
black pepper

Garnishing

1 tsp finely chopped parsley and chives
salt

Place 2 lbs of baking cheese in a linen cloth, then place it in a sieve with a weight on top. Leave to drain for a few hours.

Put the drained cheese in an ovenproof dish, sprinkle with the baking powder and mix thoroughly. Leave to stand for 2–3 hours until the cheese has gone runny.

Place the bowl of cheese over a saucepan filled with hot water. Stir the mixture constantly until the mixture is creamy and there are no lumps left (Note: make sure the temperature does not exceed 160 °F!). Remove from the heat and stir in the butter, cream and egg yolk. Add salt to taste, and leave to cool.

For the onion sauce – known in Hesse as "Music" – finely chop the onions and season with oil, vinegar, water and pepper. Stir well.

Divide the cheese among the plates, pour on the onion sauce, garnish with herbs and salt to taste.

Recipe by Mathias Fleischmann, Odenwald

Comment

Traditionally, cooked cheese is served with slices of tasty country bread, thickly spread butter and, for those who fancy something different, a sprinkling of caraway seeds.

In the Odenwald, cooked cheese is served as an "exotic" accompaniment to Bratwurst sausage or as a so-called "Kochkäseschnitzel": a breaded and fried veal scallop (Wiener Schnitzel) straight out of the pan covered with a delicious spoonfull of cooked cheese. Important: Pre-heat the serving plates!

Baking cheese (Schichtkäse) is a German speciality, it is a drier version of curd cheese.

Frankfurter Bethmännchen

Ribbelkuche

ca. 25 Stück
etwas Fett
250 g Marzipanrohmasse
 80 g Puderzucker
ca. 40 g Mehl, 1 Eiweiß
 65 g gemahlene Mandeln
 50 g ganze Mandeln, geschält, zum Verzieren
 1 Eigelb, 1 EL Wasser

Backofen auf 150 °C vorheizen. Backblech einfetten oder Backpapier verwenden. Marzipanmasse mit Puderzucker, Mehl, Eiweiß und gemahlenen Mandeln zu einem glatten Teig verkneten. Daraus ca. 25 Kugeln formen und auf das Backblech legen. Die Mandeln längs halbieren und je 3 halbe Mandeln senkrecht in jede Kugel drücken, sodass die Kugeln oben spitz werden und die typische Bethmännchen-Form erhalten. Nach Möglichkeit über Nacht kühl stellen. Das Eigelb mit Wasser verrühren und die Bethmännchen damit bestreichen. Im Backofen auf der mittleren Schiene bei Ober-Unter-Hitze 12–15 Minuten backen, bis sie eine leichte Bräunung bekommen.

Anmerkung

Bethmännchen wurden in Frankfurt für den Hausgebrauch in der Adventszeit gebacken. Sie halten sich in verschlossenen Blechdosen bis weit nach Weihnachten – wenn sie nicht schon vorher aufgegessen wurden. Als typische Frankfurter Spezialität sind sie heute jedoch das ganze Jahr über in den Konditoreien zu kaufen.
Der Rezeptursprung ist unklar. Die einen behaupten, es stamme von einem Koch der Frankfurter Familie Bethmann und die drei Mandeln stünden für die drei Söhne. Andere meinen, die drei Mandeln erinnern an betende Hände, wovon der Name (Bet-Mann) abgeleitet wurde. Wo auch immer der Ursprung liegt, absolut sicher ist, dass sie vorzüglich schmecken!

Rezept von Helga Hettler, Frankfurt

ca. 24 Stücke
500 g Weizenmehl
 80 g Zucker
 1 Prise Salz, 1 Ei
knapp ¼ l Milch
 1 Würfel frische Hefe (42 g), 80 g Butter
 1 Kunststoffschüssel mit Deckel (3 l Inhalt)

Belag
300 g Butter, 250 g Zucker
400 g Mehl
 1 Päckchen Vanillezucker (ca. 8 g)
 1 EL Semmelbrösel

Mehl in eine Schüssel sieben, eine Mulde hineindrücken, den Zucker und das Salz darüberstreuen. Das Ei und die Milch in die Mulde gießen, Hefe hineinbröseln, Butter in Flocken auf dem Mehl verteilen. Von der Mitte her alles zu einem glatten Teig verkneten. In eine angewärmte Kunststoffschüssel geben und diese mit fest sitzendem Deckel verschließen. Die Schüssel in heißes Wasser stellen, damit der Teig besser aufgeht. Wenn der Deckel aufspringt, den Teig auf einem mit Butter bestrichenen Backblech (Blechgröße ca. 35 cm × 45 cm) ausrollen. Nochmals mit einem Küchentuch zugedeckt gehen lassen, bis der Teig doppelt so dick ist. Für den Belag die Zutaten mit den Händen zu Bröseln verkneten (ribbeln) und gleichmäßig auf den Teig streuen.
Bei 200 °C 20–25 Minuten backen. Gegen Ende der Backzeit den Teig auf dem Blech an einer Ecke mit einem Messer etwas anheben. Ist der Boden des Teigs schön gebräunt, ist der Ribbelkuche fertig.

Anmerkung

Ribbel-Liebhaber nehmen um die Hälfte mehr von den Ribbelzutaten, damit der Bröselbelag schön dick wird. Den Hefeteig kann man ebenso gut – je nach Gewohnheit – nach einem Basisrezept für Hefeteig herstellen.

Rezept von Emmi Anders und Helma Goldbach, Taunus

Frankfurter Bethmännchen

approx. 25 pieces
a little butter
  8 oz raw marzipan
3½ oz powdered (confectioners') sugar
1½ oz flour, 1 egg white
2½ oz ground almonds
  2 oz whole peeled almonds for decoration
  1 egg yolk, 1 tbsp water

Preheat the oven to 300°F. Grease the baking tray or use a sheet of baking parchment.
Knead the raw marzipan, icing sugar, egg white and ground almonds to a smooth dough.
Form 25 balls and place them on the baking tray. Half the almonds and press 3 halves into the balls of dough vertically, so that the top of the ball is pointed and has the typical Bethmännchen shape. If possible, leave to stand overnight in a cool place. Mix the egg yolk with the water and glaze the Bethmännchen.
Bake on the middle shelf of the oven for 15 minutes until they are slightly brown (timing given is for convection ovens).

Comment

In the past Bethmännchen were baked in Frankfurt at home during the month of Advent. They keep well in tins until well after Christmas – that is, if they have not all been eaten by then! Bethmännchen are a typical Frankfurt specialty, and these days they can be bought all year round in confectionary stores. It is not known where the recipe comes from. Some say it originally came from a cook who worked for a Frankfurt family called the Bethmann's, and that the 3 almonds stand for their 3 sons. Other say the almonds remind you of praying hands, which is where the name "Bet-Mann" or "praying-man" comes from. Wherever they come from, one thing is for sure, they taste delicious!

Recipe by Helga Hettler, Frankfurt

Crumble Cake

makes approx. 24 slices
1 lb plain flour
3 oz sugar, 1 pinch of salt
1 egg, about 1 cup of milk
1 cube of fresh yeast (1 oz)
3 oz butter
1 plastic bowl with a lid (6 pts volume)

Topping
10½ oz butter, 8 oz sugar
14 oz plain flour
  1 packet of vanilla sugar (approx. 1½ tbsps)
  1 tbsp breadcrumbs

Sieve the flour into a bowl and make a well in the centre. Add the sugar and salt. Pour the egg and milk into the well, crumble in the yeast and add the butter in flakes.
Working from the middle, mix together to form a smooth dough. Place in a pre-warmed plastic bowl and seal tightly. Place the bowl in hot water so that the dough rises better.
Once the lid bursts open, roll out the dough on a baking tray (about 14 × 18 inches). Cover the tray with a tea towel and leave to rise until the dough has doubled in thickness.

For the topping

Mix the ingredients by hand until crumbly and spread out evenly over the base.
Bake at 400°F for 20–25 minutes.
Towards the end of the baking time, lift up a corner of the dough with a knife. If the base is brown then the "Ribbelkuche" is done.

Comment

People who love the topping use half as much again of the crumble mixture, so that it is nice and thick. The yeast dough can also be prepared according to a standard yeast dough recipe.

Recipe by Emmi Anders and Helma Goldbach, Taunus

Frankfurter Kranz
Frankfurter Kranz

Frankfurter Kranz

Frankfurter Kranz

150 g Butter, 225 g Zucker
4 Eier
1 Zitrone (Saft und Zesten)
225 g Weizenmehl, 75 g Speisestärke
¾ P. Backpulver (ca. 12 g)

Für die Form

Butter zum Ausstreichen
Ca. 100 g gemahlene Mandeln (oder Haselnüsse)

Für die Falsche Buttercreme und die Geleeschicht

¾ l Milch
2 Päckchen Vanillepudding (zum Kochen)
4 EL Zucker
48 g Kokosfett (entspricht zwei Würfeln)
300 g Butter (Zimmertemperatur)
3 EL Johannisbeergelee

Für das Krokant

20 g Butter
3 EL Zucker
300 g Mandeln (oder Haselnüsse), grob gehackt

Für die Verzierung

6 EL Johannisbeergelee

Rührteig

Backofen auf 180 °C vorheizen. Butter schaumig rühren und dabei nach und nach den Zucker einstreuen. Nach und nach ebenso die Eier und dann Zitronensaft und Zesten zugeben. Mehl und Speisestärke mischen und esslöffelweise unterrühren. Eine Kranzform mit Butter ausstreichen und mit Mandeln oder Haselnüssen ausstreuen. Den Teig einfüllen und im Backofen ca. 30–35 Minuten backen. Herausnehmen, Kuchen etwas abkühlen lassen. Den Rand mit einem Messer etwas lösen und den Kuchen auf ein Gitter stürzen und abkühlen lassen.

Falsche Buttercreme

Puddingpulver mit etwas Milch anrühren. Restliche Milch zum Kochen bringen, Vanillepudding einrühren und zweimal aufkochen lassen. Kokosfett zufügen. Dabei umrühren, damit der Pudding sich nicht am Boden festsetzt. Pudding auf Zimmertemperatur abkühlen lassen. Butter schaumig rühren und den lauwarmen Pudding esslöffelweise unterheben.

Krokant

Butter zergehen lassen, Zucker darin schmelzen und die Mandeln (Haselnüsse) darin hellbraun werden lassen. Vorsicht, sie werden sehr schnell dunkel! Die Masse heiß auf Backpapier geben, ein zweites Backpapier darüberdecken und mit der Kuchenrolle flach rollen, sodass kleinere Krokantbrösel entstehen.

Ganzer Kuchen und Verzierung

Den Kuchen mit einem Messer oder gekreuztem Faden quer in drei dicke Scheiben schneiden. Die unterste Scheibe mit 3 EL Johannisbeergelee bestreichen. Darauf etwas Buttercreme streichen. Die zweite Scheibe daraufsetzen und ebenfalls mit etwas Buttercreme bestreichen. Die oberste Scheibe aufsetzen und den ganzen Kuchen mit der restlichen Buttercreme bestreichen, etwas für die Dekoration zurückbehalten. Solange die Buttercreme noch weich ist, den Krokant daraufstreuen. Restliche Buttercreme in eine Spritztüte füllen, kleine Rosetten auf den Kuchen spritzen und auf die Spitzen einen roten Klecks Johannisbeergelee geben.

Rezept von Lilli Holl und Emmi Anders, Taunus

Petzkuche

Anmerkung

Werden die Eier in Eigelb und Eiweiß getrennt, so rührt man anfangs nur die Eigelbe unter. Das Eiweiß wird zu steifem Schnee geschlagen und erst zum Schluss vorsichtig unter den Rührteig gehoben. Dadurch wird der Kuchen lockerer.

Sollten trotz guten Ausstreichens beim Umstürzen kleine Stückchen des Kuchens in der Form hängen bleiben, was insbesondere am „Schornstein" passieren kann, löst man diese vorsichtig mit einem Messer ab und „klebt" sie mit Eiweiß wieder am Kuchen fest.

Frankfurter Kranz, klassisch

Die klassische Version des Frankfurter Kranzes wird mit Buttercreme ohne Vanillepudding, jedoch mit Rum zubereitet (siehe untenstehende Zutaten). Dann sind die Schichten dünner aufzutragen. Die Johannisbeerschicht kann entfallen.

Für die Buttercreme mit Rum

250 g Butter
4–6 EL Rum
  2 Eigelbe
150 g Puderzucker

Buttercreme mit Rum

Rum esslöffelweise in die weiche Butter schlagen, bis er vollkommen aufgenommen ist. Dann mit Eigelben und Puderzucker schaumig schlagen.

ca. 24 Stücke

500 g Weizenmehl
 80 g Zucker
  1 Prise Salz
  1 Ei
knapp ¼ l Milch
  1 Würfel frische Hefe (ca. 42 g)
 80 g Butter
  1 Kunststoffschüssel mit Deckel (3 l Inhalt)
125 g Butter
100 g Zucker
  1 TL Zimt (gestrichen)

Mehl in eine Schüssel sieben, eine Mulde hineindrücken, Zucker und Salz darüberstreuen. Ei mit Milch verquirlen und in die Mulde gießen, Hefe hineinbröseln, Butter in Flocken auf dem Mehl verteilen. Alles von der Mitte her zu einem glatten Teig verarbeiten. In eine angewärmte Kunststoffschüssel geben und mit fest sitzendem Deckel verschließen. Schüssel in heißes Wasser stellen, damit der Teig besser aufgeht. Wenn der Deckel aufspringt, den Teig auf einem mit Butter bestrichenen Backblech (Blechgröße ca. 35 cm × 45 cm) ausrollen. Nochmals mit einem Küchentuch zugedeckt gehen lassen, bis der Teig doppelt so dick ist.

Den Backofen auf 200 °C vorheizen. Inzwischen mit Daumen, Zeigefinger und Mittelfinger Dellen in den Teig petzen (zwicken). Die Butter schmelzen und wenn sie flüssig wird, mit einem Löffel auf dem Hefeteig verteilen. Dabei soll sich immer ein bisschen Butter in den Dellen sammeln.

Im Backofen 20–25 Minuten backen. Gegen Ende der Backzeit den Teig auf dem Blech an einer Ecke mit einem Messer etwas anheben. Ist der Boden des Teigs schön gebräunt, ist der Petzkuche fertig gebacken. Aus dem Backofen nehmen und noch heiß mit Zucker und Zimt bestreuen.

Rezept von Emmi Anders, Taunus

Petzkuche
Pinch Cake

Frankfurter Kranz

20–24 pieces
For the cake mixture:

5 oz butter
8 oz sugar
4 eggs
zest and juice of 1 lemon
8 oz plain flour
2½ oz cornstarch
2½ tsps baking powder

For the tin

butter to grease the tin
approx. 4 oz ground almonds (or hazelnuts)

For the "fake" buttercream and jam layer

3 cup milk
2 packets of vanilla pudding
   (the cooking variety)
4 tbsps sugar
2 oz coconut butter
10 oz butter (at room temperature)
3 tbsps blackcurrant jelly

For the brittle

¾ oz butter
3 tbsps sugar
10 oz roughly chopped almonds
   (or hazelnuts)

For the decoration

6 tbsps blackcurrant jelly

Cake mixture

Pre-heat the oven to 360°F. Beat the butter until pale and fluffy, gradually adding the sugar. Bit by bit, add the eggs and then the lemon juice and lemon zest. Mix the flour and the cornstarch. Add them to the mixture a spoon at a time.

Recipe by Lilli Holl and Emmi Anders, Taunus

Grease a Bundt pan (ring shaped baking tin) with butter and coat with the almonds. Pour in the cake mixture and bake in the oven for approx. 30–35 minutes. Remove from the oven and leave to cool for a while. Using a knife, loosen the cake from the tin and tip it out onto a wire rack. Leave to cool.

"Fake" butter cream

Mix the vanilla pudding powder with a little milk. Boil the rest of the milk and stir in the vanilla pudding mixture. Bring to the boil twice. Add the coconut fat, so that the pudding does not stick to the bottom of the pan. Allow the pudding to cool to room temperature. Beat the butter until pale and fluffy. Stir in the lukewarm vanilla pudding spoon by spoon.

Brittle

Melt the butter, then add the sugar and allow it to dissolve. Add the almonds (hazelnuts) and brown them in the pan. Be careful – they can burn very quickly!
Pour the hot mixture onto a piece of baking paper. Place a second sheet of baking paper on top and using a rolling pin, roll the mixture out flat to form small pieces of brittle.

Finishing and Decorating the Cake

Using a knife or a cake cutting wire, cut the cake horizontally into three slices.
Spread the bottom slice with 3 tablespoons of blackcurrant jelly, then spread some buttercream on top. Place the second cake slice on the top of the base and again spread some of the butter cream over it.
Finally, place the upper slice of the cake on top and cover the entire cake with a layer of butter cream, keeping a little to one side for decoration.
Whilst the buttercream is still soft, sprinkle the brittle over the cake.

Pinch Cake

Fill a piping bag with the remaining buttercream. Pipe small rosettes around the top of the cake and decorate each one with a dot of red blackcurrant jelly.

Comment

If you separate the eggs, then only add the egg yolks to the mixture to begin with. Whisk the egg whites until stiff. Once the flour has been incorporated into the mixture, carefully fold in the egg whites. The cake mixture is lighter if it is made this way.

If some of the cake sticks to the tin when you turn it out, which is often the case at the narrowest part of the ring, loosen it from the tin carefully using a knife, and "glue" it back on the cake with egg white.

Traditional Frankfurter Kranz

For the traditional version of Frankfurter Kranz, the buttercream is made without vanilla pudding but with rum (see ingredients below). The layers of butter cream are thinner and the layer of blackcurrant jelly can be left out.

For the Buttercream with Rum

2 egg yolks
6 tbsps rum
8 oz butter
4 oz powdered (confectioners') sugar

Buttercream with Rum

Beat the rum into the butter, one spoon at a time, until there is none left. Then add the egg yolk and sugar and beat until fluffy.

.

approx. 24 pieces

1 lb plain flour
3 oz sugar
1 pinch of salt
1 egg
about a 1 cup of milk
1 fresh cube of yeast (1 oz)
3 oz butter
1 plastic bowl with a lid (6 pts volume)
4 oz butter
4 oz sugar
1 level tsp cinnamon

Sieve the flour into a bowl and make a well in the centre. Add the sugar and salt. Pour the egg and milk into the well, crumble in the yeast and add the butter in flakes.

Working from the middle, mix together to form a smooth dough. Place in a pre-warmed plastic bowl and seal tightly. Place the bowl in hot water so that the dough rises better.

Once the lid bursts open, roll out the dough on a baking tray that has been greased with butter (about 14 × 18 inches). Cover the tray with a tea towel and leave to rise until the dough has doubled in thickness.

Pre-heat the oven to 400 °F

Using your thumb, index finger and middle finger, pinch bumps into the dough. Melt the butter and spoon it over the dough. There should always be a little more butter in the "bumps".

Bake in the oven for approx. 20–25 minutes. Towards the end of the baking time lift one corner of the dough from the baking tray. If the base is brown, the pinch cake is done.

Remove from the oven and sprinkle with cinnamon and sugar whilst still warm.

Recipe by Emmi Anders, Taunus

Schmandcreme mit Himbeeren
Heavy Sour Cream with Raspberries

Schmandcreme mit Himbeeren

½ l Schmand
200 g Zucker
etwas kaltes Wasser
8 g weiße Gelatine
1 Vanillestange
250 g Himbeeren
3 EL Zucker
4 Minzeblättchen

Schmand mit Zucker 10 Minuten schaumig schlagen. Gelatine in etwas Wasser einweichen. Vanillestange längs aufschneiden und das Vanillemark mit einem Messer herausschaben. Unter den Schmand rühren. Die eingeweichte Gelatine gut ausdrücken. 2–3 EL Wasser heiß werden lassen und die Gelatine dazugeben. So lange rühren, bis sie sich aufgelöst hat. Die Flüssigkeit unter Rühren nach und nach zu dem Schmand geben. Die Schmandcreme in 4 Dessertgläser füllen und einige Stunden kalt stellen.
Vier schöne Himbeeren für die Dekoration zurückbehalten, die übrigen pürieren. Zucker unterrühren. Himbeerpüree als oberste Schicht auf die Schmandcreme geben. Jeweils mit einer Himbeere und je einem Minzeblättchen dekorieren.

Rezept von Hans-Jost Knauf, Schwalm

Hoing – Zwetschenmus auf Taunus-Art

ca. 8 Gläser (à 500 ml)
5 kg Zwetschen
½ Tasse Wasser
500 g Zucker
etwas Zimt
etwas Sternanis, gemahlen

Zwetschen waschen, entkernen und in einen Bräter füllen. Wasser dazugießen, Bräter mit einem Deckel gut verschließen und die Früchte im Backofen 1 Stunde bei 200 °C garen lassen. Währenddessen den Bräter nicht öffnen und nicht umrühren. Die Temperatur des Backofens auf 150 °C reduzieren. Den Deckel abnehmen und Mus, das sich an den Seitenwänden angesetzt hat, mit einem flachen Schaber abkratzen. Zucker, Zimt und Sternanis unterrühren und offen weitere 2 Stunden köcheln lassen. Immer wieder das Mus von den Topfseiten abkratzen und unterrühren.
In der Zwischenzeit die Einmachgläser sehr heiß ausspülen und auf einem sauberen Küchentuch mit der Öffnung nach unten trocknen lassen. Nicht abtrocknen, damit sie weitestgehend steril bleiben. Wenn das Mus die gewünschte Konsistenz erreicht hat, mithilfe eines Trichters heiß in die Einmachgläser füllen.

Anmerkung

Der Hesse liebt das Mus heute auf frischem Roggenmischbrot mit Butter. Früher war es Bestandteil eines üblichen Nachtessens: Quellkartoffeln (Pellkartoffeln) mit „Hoing" und Schmierkäs (Quark). Eine köstliche Abwechslung für die fleischlose Küche! *Zwetschen* werden regional unterschiedlich auch *Zwetschgen* oder *Zwetschken* genannt. Alle gehören zur *Familie der Pflaumen* und unterscheiden sich vor allem in der Größe und Reifezeit. Wer den „Hoing" andernorts nachkochen will, kann also getrost auch andere Sorten verwenden.

Rezept von Berta Schmidt, Taunus

Heavy Sour Cream with Raspberries

1 pint heavy sour cream
8 oz sugar
a little cold water
1½ tsp white gelatin
1 vanilla pod
9 oz raspberries
3 tbsps sugar
4 mint leaves

Beat the sugar and the sour cream for
10 minutes until fluffy. Soak the gelatin in
water.
Slice the vanilla pod open lengthwise and scrape
out the seeds with the knife. Stir into the sour
cream. Squeeze out the soaked gelatin. Heat
2–3 tbsp water, add the gelatin and stir until it
dissolves. Keep stirring and add the liquid to
the sour cream bit by bit. Fill the mixture into
4 dessert glasses and chill for a few hours.
Put 4 good raspberries aside for the garnish,
puree the rest. Stir in the sugar. Pour the raspberry
puree over the sour cream. Garnish each glass
with one raspberry and a mint leaf.

Recipe by Hans-Jost Knauf, Schwalm

Taunus Style Plum Puree

makes about 8 jars (1 pint)
11 lbs plums, ½ cup of water
1 lb sugar
some cinnamon and ground star anise

Wash and stone the plums. Put them in a roasting
dish and add the water. Cover with a close fitting
lid, place in the oven and leave to cook for 1 hour
at 400°F. (Do not open the dish or stir during the
cooking time). Reduce the oven temperature to
300°F.
Remove the lid and scrape off any fruit pulp
that has stuck to the sides of the dish with a flat
spatula.
Stir in the sugar, cinnamon and star anise and
leave to simmer for a further 2 hours. Scrape the
fruit pulp from the sides of the dish at regular
intervals and give the mixture a good stir.
In the meantime, rinse out the jars with very
hot water and leave them to dry upside down on
a clean tea towel. To keep them as sterile as
possible, do not dry them by hand.
When the fruit pulp has reached the desired
consistency fill it into the jars using a funnel.

Comment

These days, people in Hesse enjoy plum puree
with fresh rye bread and butter. In the past, it
formed part of the evening meal: boiled potatoes
with "Hoing" and curd cheese (quark). It makes
a delicious change as a vegetarian meal.
Depending on the region, "Zwetschen" (plums)
are known variously as "Zwetschgen" or
"Zwetschken". All varieties belong to the plum
family, the greatest differences being size and
ripening season. So, if you want to make "Hoing",
but live somewhere else, don't worry, you can use
other plum varieties!

Recipe by Berta Schmidt, Taunus

Äppelwoi
Hessian Cider

Apfelwein
Anleitung zur Herstellung von Äppelwoi

ca. 30 Liter Apfelwein

1 Gärgefäß (30 l: Kunststoffbehälter mit Ablasshahn und Deckel oder ein Glasballon mit Gummistopfen und Gärröhrchen)

30 l frischer Apfelmost (Süßer)

30 saubere Flaschen (à 1 l) mit Verschluss oder Korken

Das saubere Gärgefäß an einen dunklen Ort stellen. Den Most durch einen Perlonfilter hinein gießen, um grobe Trübstoffe zurück zu behalten. Das Gefäß nur bis zu 90% füllen, damit genügend Platz für die Gärung bleibt. Den Deckel bzw. den Gummistopfen nach Anweisung des Herstellers mit dem Gärröhrchen ausstatten und das Gärgefäß verschließen. Darauf achten, dass aus dem Gärröhrchen Luft entweichen kann. Apfelmost (Süßer) gärt optimal bei einer Temperatur um die 20 °C. Bei der ersten Gärung rauscht es kräftig im Behälter, weshalb die Hessen den gärenden Most in diesem Stadium als Rauscher bezeichnen. Wenn es nach einigen Monaten im Röhrchen nicht mehr gluckert und blubbert, ist der Apfelwein fertig. Das dauert von der Mostherstellung im September/Oktober etwa bis Weihnachten. Das *Stöffche* (fertiger Apfelwein) nun vom Bodensatz abziehen, weil der Satz Aussehen und Geschmack beeinträchtigt. Vorsichtig durch den Hahn oder mit einem Schlauch in Flaschen füllen und den trüben Bodensatz zurück lassen. Die Flaschen bis zum Rand füllen, damit so wenig Sauerstoff wie möglich in der Flasche verbleibt, und verschließen. Wichtig ist nun eine kühle Lagerung bei konstanten 10–14 °C, um die Haltbarkeit zu gewährleisten und die Selbstklärung zu ermöglichen. Trinken sollte man den Äppelwoi innerhalb von 6–8 Wochen, wenn er sein volles Aroma hat.

Anmerkung

Bei allen Arbeitsschritten auf äußerste Sauberkeit achten!

Fertigen, frisch gepressten Apfelmost gibt es bei Lohnkeltereien. Der Most besteht aus einer Mischung verschiedenster Äpfel. Wer Most von den eigenen Äpfeln verwenden will, geht zu kleineren Lohnkeltereien, in denen der Most auch noch von den mitgebrachten, eigenen Äpfeln gekeltert wird.

Alte Sorten von Hochstammbäumen wie Schafsnase, Rheinischer Bohnapfel, Trierer Weinapfel etc. verwenden.

Tafelobst wie Granny Smith, Breaburn, Golden Delicious etc. enthält zu wenige Aromastoffe und ist für ein gutes „Stöffche" ungeeignet.

Für die regelmäßige Heimproduktion von Apfelmost lohnt sich die Anschaffung einer kleinen Obstmühle und einer Obstpresse (Spindelpresse). Die Äpfel in der Mühle zuerst zerkleinern und dann auspressen.

Faustregel: 50 kg Äpfel ergeben, in Keltereien gepresst, ca. 30 l Most, selbst gepresste Äpfel in der Regel 10–15 l Most.

Keine faulen Äpfel, nur reifes, gesundes Obst verwenden.

Die Ausrüstung ist in Drogerien, im Fachhandel oder über das Internet erhältlich.

Rezept von Heinz Peter, Vordertaunus

Instructions
for making cider

makes approx. 8 gallons of cider

1 fermentation tank, 8 gallons volume
  (plastic tank with lid and tap,
  or glass demijohn with rubber cork
  and fermentation lock)
8 gallons freshly pressed apple juice
30 clean bottles (2 pts) with a screw top or cork

Stand the clean fermentation tank in a dark place. Pour the apple juice into the tank through a Perlon filter to remove any large particles. Do not fill the container more than 90% full, so that enough space remains for the fermentation process.

Fit the lid or rubber stopper with the fermentation lock in accordance with the manufacturer's instructions. Close the lid ensuring that air can escape. Apple juice ferments best at temperatures around 70°F.

During the initial fermentation phase, the juice makes a loud hissing, bubbling noise known in German as "rauschen". That's why, in Hesse, it is called "Rauscher" at this stage of the process. After a few months, when the bubbling and gurgling noises can no longer be heard in the tube, the cider is ready. This generally takes from September/ October, when the apple juice is made, until Christmas.

Drain off the "Stöffche"(finished cider) from the sediment or it will impair the taste and appearance of the cider.

Carefully siphon off into bottles using a tube or the tap, ensuring the sediment remains in the container.

Fill the bottles to the rim, so that as little oxygen remains in the bottle as possible, and seal.

It is important to store the cider in a cool place at a constant temperature of between 50°F – 57°F. This aids the clarifying process and prolongs the shelf life.

The "Stöffche" is best consumed within 6–8 weeks while it still has its full aroma.

Comment

Strict hygiene is of the utmost importance at all stages of the process!

Ready made, freshly pressed apple juice is available at commercial cider makers.

The juice is made from a mixture of various apples. If you want to use juice from your own apples, you should go to one of the smaller commercial cider makers, where apple juice can be made from apples you bring yourself.

Use older sorts of apples from the taller rootstocks such as the Schafsnase, Rheinischer Bohnapfel, Trierer Weinapfel etc. Dessert fruit, like Granny Smith, Braeburn, Golden Delicious etc. do not contain sufficient aromatic substances and are not suitable for making "Stöffche".

If you intend to make your own cider regularly, it is worth purchasing a small revolving fruit mill and press.

Mill the apples first before you press them.

As a rough guide: 110 lbs of apples yield about 8 gallons of juice if pressed at a commercial cider maker. Home-pressed apples yield about 3–4 gallons.

Do not use rotten apples. Only use ripe and healthy fruit.

A cider making kit can be purchased in most pharmacies, specialist shops and via the internet.

Recipe by Heinz Peter, Vordertaunus

Aufgesetzter Dauborner Schlehenlikör

ergibt 1 Liter

   1 kg Schlehen
   1 l Dauborner Doppelkorn (38 Vol.-%)
   1 Vanillestange
250 g Zucker

Schlehen nach dem ersten Frost vom Strauch pflücken. Die Beeren gut verlesen, alle Stiele entfernen und kurz unter fließendem Wasser abspülen. Beeren abtrocknen und in ein sauberes Gefäß füllen. Vanillestange der Länge nach aufschneiden, das Mark herauskratzen und mit dem Zucker vermischen. Über die Beeren streuen und mit dem Doppelkorn übergießen. Gefäß gut verschließen und an einem schattigen, warmen Ort 6–8 Wochen stehen lassen, bis die Beeren blass geworden sind. Den Likör durch ein feines Sieb (Kaffeefilter) abgießen. In Flaschen umfüllen und sehr gut verschließen, damit der Alkohol nicht verdunstet.

Anmerkung

Das kleine Dorf Dauborn im Landkreis Limburg-Weilburg ist weithin bekannt für seine jahrhundertealte Kornbrennertradition. Der Ursprung liegt im benachbarten Kloster Gnadenthal. Das Fürstentum Oranien-Nassau richtete hier 1656 eine Kornbrennerei ein. Dauborner Einwohner, die im Kloster ihre Dienste verrichteten, erlernten dabei das Schnapsbrennverfahren und brachten es in ihr Heimatdorf. Der Jahresausstoß aller Dauborner Brennereien wird für die Mitte des 19. Jahrhunderts auf 500 000 Liter reinen Alkohol geschätzt. Derzeit produzieren die übrig gebliebenen sechs Brennereien vermutlich rund 40 000 Liter.

Hinweis

Für die Herstellung von Aufgesetztem werden gerne alle heimischen Beeren wie Johannisbeeren, Himbeeren, Blaubeeren oder Preiselbeeren verwendet. Wer Quitte gerne mag, schält und entkernt sie vorher und schneidet das Fruchtfleisch klein, damit Geschmack und Aroma besser austreten können.
Je hochprozentiger der Korn ist, desto weniger schmeckt der Likör nach Alkohol. Deshalb wird in Dauborn mindestens 38%iger Doppelkorn verwendet.
Bei säuerlichen Beeren – und wenn gerne besonders süßer Likör getrunken wird – können ganz nach Belieben bis zu 500 g Zucker zugefügt werden. Kandiszucker, weiß oder braun, verleiht noch einen besonderen Geschmack.

Rezept von Bettina Wagner, Dauborn

Sloe Liqueur

makes 2 pints

2 lbs sloes
2 pts Dauborner double distilled wheat
    schnapps (38 % alcohol)
1 vanilla pod
8 oz sugar

Pick the sloes from the bush after the first winter
frost.
Sort the berries carefully and remove the stems. Rinse
them quickly under running water, then dry the
berries and place them in a clean container. With
a sharp knife, cut the vanilla pod open lengthwise.
Remove the seeds and mix them with the sugar.
Sprinkle the vanilla sugar over the berries and
pour in the schnapps. Seal the container well and
leave it to stand in a warm, shady place for 6–8
weeks until the berries have gone pale. Filter the
liqueur with a fine sieve or coffee filter. Decant into bottles and make sure that they are closed
tightly to prevent the alcohol from evaporating.

Comment

The small village of Dauborn, in the county of
Limburg-Weilburg, is widely known for its
traditional schnapps distilleries which go back
centuries.
Their origins can be traced back to the nearby
monastery, "Kloster Gnadenthal". The principality
of Oranien-Nassau founded a schnapps distillery
there in 1656. The inhabitants of Dauborn who
worked there learned the distillery process and
took their knowledge back to their home village.
In the mid 19th century, the combined annual
production of all of the distilleries in Dauborn is
estimated to have been over 1 000 000 pints of pure
alcohol. These days, the remaining 6 breweries
probably produce about 85 000 pints.

Note

Any berries that can be found locally, e. g.
blackcurrants, raspberries, blueberries or
cranberries can be used to make this type
of liqueur. If you like quinces, remove the core
first and then cut the flesh into small pieces,
so that the flavor and aroma can seep out more
easily.
The higher the alcohol content of the schnapps,
the less the liqueur will taste of alcohol. That's
why in Dauborn they use at least 38% double
distilled wheat schnapps.
For sour tasting berries – or if the liqueur should
be particularly sweet – you can add up to 1 lb of
sugar extra. Rock sugar gives the liqueur a special
note.

Recipe by Bettina Wagner, Dauborn

Bouillon

Gemüsebrühe

Standardrezept für 1 l Brühe
500 g Rinderknochen, davon 3 Markknochen
1½ l Wasser
1 Bd. Suppengrün
1 Zwiebel

Die Knochen gut waschen, damit alle Knochen-
splitter abgespült werden. In einen großen Topf
geben. Kaltes Wasser dazugießen und zum Kochen
bringen. Bei geringer Wärmezufuhr ca. 2½ Stunden
sieden lassen.
Das Suppengrün putzen und waschen. Die Möhre
ganz lassen, Lauch in ca. 6 cm lange Stücke und
Knollensellerie in grobe Würfel schneiden. Zwiebel
putzen, die Schale nicht entfernen.
Das Suppengrün mit der ungeschälten ganzen
Zwiebel 40 Minuten vor Ende der Kochzeit in die
Fleischbrühe geben. Schaum, der sich durch das
gerinnende Eiweiß bildet, zwischendurch immer
wieder mit einer Schaumkelle abschöpfen.
Nach der Kochzeit die Brühe durch ein feines Sieb
schütten. Das Mark aus den Knochen lösen, sehr
klein schneiden und in die Brühe geben.
Die Fleischbrühe weiterverwenden für Suppen,
Eintöpfe oder Soßen. Als Vorrat schnell abkühlen
und in einem verschlossenen Behälter kühl aufbewahren, damit sie nicht sauer wird.

Anmerkung

Reichhaltiger wird die Fleischbrühe (und verdient
dann auch ihren Namen), wenn zu den Knochen
ein Stück Suppenfleisch, ca. 500 g, mitgekocht
wird. Fleisch und Gemüse werden meist nicht
weiterverwendet. Es kann aber sehr klein geschnitten auch als Einlage zu einer Nudelsuppe
oder in einen Eintopf gegeben werden.
Sinnvoll ist es, die Brühe als Basis ohne Salz und
Gewürze zuzubereiten, um ein späteres Über-
würzen zu verhindern. So kann dann die fertige
Speise nach ihrer individuellen Geschmacksrichtung jeweils mit den passenden Gewürzen und
der entsprechenden Menge Salz abgeschmeckt
werden.

Standardrezept für 1 l Brühe
1 Zwiebel
je 2 Stangen Lauch und Staudensellerie
1 große Kartoffel, 2 Möhren
1 Petersilienwurzel
2 EL Sonnenblumenöl
2 Lorbeerblätter
150 ml trockener Weißwein
1 l Wasser

Gemüse putzen, waschen und in Scheiben schneiden. Öl heiß werden lassen und Zwiebel, Lauch,
Sellerie und Kartoffel darin bei geringer Wärmezufuhr ca. 10 Minuten andünsten. Karotten, Petersilienwurzel und Lorbeerblätter zufügen, mit Weißwein auffüllen und mit dem Gemüse verrühren.
Ca. 2 Minuten kochen lassen, bis der Alkohol verdunstet ist. Wasser zugießen und erneut aufkochen. Bei geringer Wärmezufuhr zugedeckt
1 Stunde köcheln lassen.
Die Brühe durch ein Sieb abgießen. Das Gemüse
gut auspressen, damit alle Geschmacksstoffe in
die Brühe gehen. Diese nochmals durch ein feines
Sieb abseihen.
Zum Kochen wie gewohnt weiterverwenden. Als
Vorrat schnell abkühlen lassen und zugedeckt kalt
aufbewahren. Haltbar im Kühlschrank ca. 2 Tage,
tiefgefroren bis zu 3 Monate.

Anmerkung

Je nach Belieben können die Zutaten mit anderen
Gemüsesorten ergänzt oder ausgetauscht werden.
Kohl oder Fenchel sind aber mit Bedacht zu verwenden, da sie den Geschmack der Brühe sehr domi-
nieren und nicht zu allen Gerichten passen.
Auch hier ist es gut, die Brühe als Basis ohne Salz
und Gewürze zuzubereiten, um ein späteres Über-
würzen zu verhindern. Die fertige Speise kann so
nach ihrer individuellen Geschmacksrichtung mit
den passenden Gewürzen und der entsprechenden Menge Salz abgeschmeckt werden.

Meat stock

Vegetable stock

Basic recipe for 2 pts of stock

1 lb beef bones – of which 3 marrow bones
3 pts water
1 bunch of greens
1 onion

Wash the bones thoroughly to rinse off any bone splinters. Place in a large saucepan. Add the cold water and bring to the boil. Simmer gently for 2½ hours.
Sort and wash the greens. Leave the carrots whole. Cut the leeks into 2 inch pieces. Roughly dice the celeriac. Clean the onions, but do not remove the skins.
40 minutes before the stock has finished cooking, add the greens and the whole, unpeeled onions. Regularly remove any froth formed by the congealing protein with a ladle.
Once the stock has finished simmering, pour it through a fine sieve. Free the marrow from the bones and chop very finely. Add to the stock.
Use the stock for soups, stews or sauces.
To store, cool quickly and store chilled in a sealed container to prevent it from turning sour.

Comment

The meat stock is richer (and deserves its name too) if a piece of boiling meat (approx. 1 lb) is added to the bones. The meat and the vegetables are not normally used once they have been removed from the stock. They can, however, be chopped finely and added to clear noodle soups or stews.
It is advisable to prepare the stock without salt or pepper to avoid over-seasoning later.
It is generally best to season dishes individually with the appropriate herbs and spices, adding the right amount of salt as required.

Basic recipe for 2 pts of vegetable stock

1 onion
2 leeks
2 sticks of celery
1 large potato
2 carrots
1 parsley root
2 tbps sunflower oil
2 bay leaves
5 fl oz dry white wine
2 pts water

Clean and wash the vegetables. Cut into slices. Heat the oil and gently cook the onions, leeks, celery and potato for about 10 minutes. Add the carrots, parsley root and bay leaves. Pour in the white wine and stir well. Boil for about 2 minutes until the alcohol has evaporated. Add the water and bring back to the boil. Simmer gently for 1 hour.
Pour the stock through a sieve. Squeeze out the vegetables well to release the flavor. Pour through a fine sieve once again.
Use to cook as required.
To store, cool quickly and keep chilled in a sealed container. Keeps in the fridge for 2 days, up to 3 months in the freezer.

Comment

Other vegetables can be used as desired. Be careful when using cabbage or fennel, they tend to dominate the taste of the stock, and are not suitable for all meals.
It is a good idea to prepare the basic stock without salt and pepper to avoid over-seasoning later. It is generally best to season dishes individually with the appropriate herbs and spices, adding the right amount of salt as required.

Hessische Impressionen
Impressions of Hesse

Die Vergangenheit Hessens ist bewegt. Bis in die Zeit der germanischen Chatten, der Römer und des Heiligen Bonifatius reicht die Geschichte. Es gäbe keinen Wein in Hessen, wenn es den Römern zwischen 100 v. Chr. und 400 n. Chr. nicht gelungen wäre, am Rhein die Herrschaft zu erlangen. Die Reben brachten sie aus Rom mit, um ihren Wein auch im germanischen Barbarenland trinken zu können. Der Limes, ehemals römischer Grenzwall und von der UNESCO zum Weltkulturerbe ernannt, bildete die Grenze zwischen dem Römischen Reich und den Germanischen Stammesgebieten in der Zeit von 100 bis 260 n. Chr. Der Wall war Teil der 5000 km langen Befestigung Roms, die sich von Britannien quer durch Europa und den Mittleren Osten bis nach Nordafrika zog. Der Limes in Hessen lässt sich von Holzhausen im westlichen Taunus durch die Wetterau bis hinunter in den Odenwald verfolgen. Das Römerkastell Saalburg, in der Nähe von Bad Homburg, ist als einziges von ehemals 60 größeren Kastellen am Obergermanisch-Raetischen Limes vollständig rekonstruiert worden. Es lädt Besucher ein, sich auf anschauliche und lebendige Weise über die römische Geschichte und Kultur sowie über den Limes zu informieren.

Von Oberhessen aus vollzog sich nach Beendigung der Römerzeit die Christianisierung Deutschlands durch die Missionierung des Bonifatius. Es folgten 400 Jahre, in denen alle Teile des heutigen Hessens unter der Führung der Merowinger und Karolinger vereint waren. Dann zerfiel das Gebiet für 1000 Jahre in viele Einzelterritorien, bis die Landgrafschaft Hessen stark genug wurde, die politische Führung und damit die Führung des Protestantismus zu übernehmen, was später vom Haus Nassau-Dillenburg fortgesetzt wurde. Der Dreißigjäh-

rige Krieg, Angriffe Ludwigs XIV., die französische Revolution und die Kriege Napoleons folgten und hinterließen ihre Spuren, auch sprachlich und in der Küche. Wenn de Madam (franz. Madame) von Gruschelbeern (franz. grosseille) babbelt (franz. babiler), ist die Gattin gemeint, die etwas von Johannisbeeren daherschwatzt. Das heutige Hessen entstand 1945 aus dem Volksstaat Hessen und den beiden preußischen Provinzen Kurhessen und Nassau. Nach dem 2. Weltkrieg zogen die US-Amerikaner die Grenzen, wie sie noch heute bestehen.

Die Geschichte hat dem Land viele Burgen und Schlösser beschert. Eine reizvolle Burgenlandschaft erstreckt sich von Bad Karlshafen im Norden bis nach Hirschhorn im südlichsten Zipfel. Die zum Teil auf eine 1000-jährige Geschichte zurückblickenden Bauten waren Schauplatz historischer Ereignisse und Wirkungsstätte bekannter Persönlichkeiten. Sie sind heute oftmals noch eindrucksvolle Anlagen, die Besuchern gerne ihre Tore, Küchen und Keller öffnen.

Wer die Bevölkerung in den nördlichen, althessischen Gebieten kennt, wird sie wohl eher als verharrend und zurückhaltend beschreiben. In den südlichen, fränkisch bestimmten, reicheren Teilen Hessens, in denen auch die Römer stärker ihre Spuren hinterließen, sind die Menschen zugänglicher und offener. Hier wirkt sich der Einfluss größerer Städte, die damals im übrigen Hessen fast fehlten, schon seit der Römerzeit aus. Bereits im Jahr 1240 verlieh Kaiser Friedrich II. der Stadt Frankfurt das Privileg zur Durchführung von Messen. Diese brachten über die nächsten Jahrhunderte Reichtum und Wohlstand durch internationalen Handel mit chinesischen Seidenstoffen, orientalischen Gewürzen und vielem mehr. Kein Wunder also, dass die Frankfurter Küche schon in frühen Jahrhunderten einen phänomenalen Ruf besaß. Gasthöfe in Frankfurt waren weit in den europäischen Raum hinein für ihre Köstlichkeiten berühmt.

In jeder Epoche der deutschen Literaturgeschichte haben bedeutende Dichterpersönlichkeiten in Hessen gewirkt. Als älteste überlieferte germanische Heldendichtung in althochdeutscher Sprache gilt das Hildebrandslied, das im 9. Jahrhundert im Kloster Fulda aufgezeichnet wurde. Die Reihe wird mit dem bedeutendsten Romanautor des Barock, Hans Jakob Christoffel von Grimmelshausen, fortgesetzt. Er beschrieb seine Erlebnisse und Ereignisse aus dem Dreißigjährigen Krieg. Internationalen Rang erzielten die in Hanau geborenen Gebrüder Grimm, die durch die Aufzeichnung ihrer Sagen- und Märchensammlung berühmt wurden. Ihre Kinder- und Hausmärchen haben inzwischen den Rang eines UNESCO-Weltdokumentenerbes. Johann Wolfgang von Goethe, Hessens berühmtester Sohn, wurde mitten in Frankfurt geboren. Hier wuchs er auf, hier ist der Schauplatz seines großen Romans „Dichtung und Wahrheit", seiner Autobiografie der Jahre 1749 bis 1775. Weiter in die Namensliste der Literaten reihen sich ein: Georg Christoph Lichtenberg, erster großer Meister des Aphorismus und der Satire in Deutschland, Clemens Brentano, Achim von Arnim, Ludwig Börne, Karl Georg Büchner, Carl Zuckmayer, Elisabeth Langgässer und viele mehr.

Beflügelt wurden diese großen Geister vielleicht vom Nationalgetränk der Hessen, dem Apfelwein. Er kann mit Recht als das bekannteste Produkt des Landes bezeichnet werden. Überall dort, wo aufgrund des Klimas oder des Bodens die Traubenherstellung schwierig war, hat sich der Obstanbau durchgesetzt. Streuobstwiesen sind ein typisches Merkmal in den breiten hessischen Senken und so liegt es nahe, dass sich eine regelrechte Kultur des Apfelweins entwickeln konnte. Am liebsten wird er im Süd- und Mittelhessischen, im Frankfurter Raum und in Unterfranken getrunken. Dort heißt er dann Äppelwoi, Ebbelwoi, Äbbelwoi, Ebbelwei oder auch Stöffche. Traditionsgerecht wird er im Bembel auf den Tisch gestellt und vorzugsweise aus speziellen Gläsern, den Gerippten (siehe Abbildung Seite 74/75), getrunken. Alteingesessene Frankfurter trinken nicht einfach nur ihren Apfelwein. Äppelwoi, den „petzt mer", den „robbt mer" oder „mer baaft'n". Wer zum ersten Mal Apfelwein trinkt, wird sich vielleicht schütteln, weil der Schoppe durchaus herb oder gar sauer überraschen kann.

In Hessen wird gern und oft gefeiert. Unterschiedlichste kulturelle Veranstaltungen im ganzen Land machen es lebens- und besuchenswert: Zum Beispiel laden das Rheingau-Musik-Festival, die Bad Hersfelder Festspiele, die Weilburger Schlosskonzerte, das Frankfurter Museumsuferfest, der Hessentag, die documenta in Kassel, viele Volksfeste mit ihren historischen Wurzeln, über 300 private und öffentliche Museen und vieles mehr auch ein verwöhntes Publikum zum Entdecken, Entspannen und Genießen ein.

„Ei, komme se doch emal gugge!"

Hesse has an eventful history that can be traced back to the ancient Germanic Chatti tribes, the Romans and Saint Boniface. There would be no wine in Hessen had the Romans not gained control of the Rhine between 100 B. C and 400 A. D. They brought vines with them from Rome so that they could continue to enjoy their wine despite the fact that they were living in the land of the Germanic barbarians.

The Limes, a former boundary wall that has been declared a World Heritage site by UNESCO, marked the border between the Roman Empire and the Germanic tribes in the period from 100 A. D. to 260 A. D. The wall was part of the approximately 3000 mile long fortification of Rome that ran from Britain, right across Europe and the Middle East to North Africa.

The Limes can be followed from Holzhausen, in the western part of the Taunus, through the Wetterau down to the Odenwald. Of the 60 larger forts located on the Upper Germanic & Rhaetian Limes, the Saalburg, a Roman fort situated near Bad Homburg, is the only one that has been completely reconstructed. It presents visitors with a vivid and informative picture of Roman history and culture, and invites them to learn about the Limes. After the fall of the Roman Empire, St Boniface's missionary work began in Upper Hesse and the Christianization of Germany spread from here to the rest of the country. In the 400 years that followed, the regions that make up modern day Hesse were united under the leadership of the Merovingians and the Carolings.

After this period, the region fragmented into numerous small territories for about a thousand years, until the Landgraves had become strong enough to take over political leadership. At the same time, they took over leadership of the Protestant Church, which later passed to the House of Nassau-Dillenburg.

The 30 Years War, attacks by Ludwig XIV, the French Revolution and the Napoleonic Wars all followed, leaving their mark both in the language and in the cuisine. For example, when: "*de Madam* (French – Madame) *von Gruschelbeern* (French – groseilles) *babbelt* (French – babiler)" – then "the lady of the house" is meant, who is "babbling on about black-currants."

Modern Hesse was born of the People's State of Hessen and the two Prussian provinces of Kurhessen and Nassau. After the Second World War, the US Americans drew the borders which remain unchanged to this day.

History has given the state many castles and palaces. An attractive countryside, dotted with castles, stretches from Bad Karlshafen, in the north, to Hirschhorn, which is located in the most southerly tip.

Some of the buildings have a history that dates back 1000 years. They were the venues for important historical events and where famous people lived and worked. To this day, many of them remain impressive buildings and are happy to open their gates, kitchens and cellars to the public.

Anyone who knows the people in the northern and oldest parts of Hesse would describe them as persistent and reserved. In the wealthier southern regions of Hesse, where both the Frankish influence and the legacy of the Romans can be felt, the people are mostly more approachable and open.

The influence of larger cities has played a role here since as far back as Roman times, when most of the rest of Hesse lacked any larger towns.

As early as 1240, Emperor Friedrich II awarded the city of Frankfurt the right to host trade fairs. For the few hundred years that followed, these brought wealth and prosperity to the city in the form of international trade in silk from China, oriental spices and many other items.

It's hardly surprising then, that Frankfurt's cuisine had such a phenomenally good reputation so early on. The inns here were famous all throughout Europe for their delicacies.

In every era of German literature, important writers and poets were active in Hesse. The oldest surviving record of Germanic epic poetry is the "Hildebrandslied" that was recorded in the 9th Century, at the monastery of Fulda. The list was continued by the most important Baroque author, Hans Jakob Christoffel von Grimmelshausen, who described his experiences and the events of the Thirty Years War.

The Brothers Grimm, who were born in Hanau, gained international renown when they recorded their collection of legends and fairy tales. These days, their "Children's and Household Tales" are part of the UNESCO World Documentary Heritage.

Johann Wolfgang Goethe, Hesse's most famous citizen, was born and raised in the centre of Frankfurt. He set his great book here, "Dichtung und Wahrheit" (Poetry and Truth), an autobiography of the period from 1749 to 1775.

Other names on the list of great writers from the region are: Georg Christoph Lichtenberg, the first great master of aphorism and satire in Germany, Clemens Brentano, Achim von Arnim, Ludwig Börne, Karl Georg Büchner, Carl Zuckmayer, Elisabeth Langgässer and many more.

These great minds were perhaps inspired by Hesse's national drink – apple cider. It can justifiably be called the best known product in the region.

Wherever the climate or the soil made it difficult to grow vines, fruit trees took over. Meadows dotted with fruit trees are a typical feature of Hesse's wide valleys, so it is not surprising that a real cider culture developed.

It is most popular in Southern and Middle Hesse, around Frankfurt and in Lower Franken, where it is known either as *Ebbelwoi, Äbbelwoi, Ebbelwei* or *Stöffche*. In accordance with the tradition, it should be served in an earthenware jug called a *Bembel* which is placed on the table. The cider is then drunk from special glasses called a *Gerippten* (glass beakers engraved with a diamond shaped pattern that refracts the light, see page 74/75).

Long-established locals in Frankfurt do not simply "drink" their cider. They have at least three different words to say what they do with it!

Äbbelwoi can be *petzt, robbt* or *baaft*. Anyone drinking apple cider for the first time may shudder after the first mouthful. The *Schoppe* can be surprisingly dry or even sour.

In Hessen, people like to celebrate a lot. Numerous cultural events throughout the state make it a wonderful place to live and one worth visiting. For example: the Rheingau-Music-Festival, the Bad Hersfelder Festspiele, the Weilburger Schlosskonzerte, the Frankfurter Museumsuferfest, the Hessentag, the documenta in Kassel, lots of folk festivals with their historical roots, over 300 public and private museums and many other things mean that the public are spoilt for choice when it comes to deciding how to relax, what to enjoy and which of the many new things they would like to discover here.

So, as they say here … *"Ei, komme se doch emal gugge!"* Come and check us out!

Regionale Spezialitäten und Genüsse aus Deutschland

Original Badisch –
The Best of Baden Food
von Monika Graff und
Heidi Knoblich, 73 Seiten,
deutsch/englisch,
ISBN 3-7750-0416-5.
Die Badische Küche und ihr
Wein sind weit über ihre Gren-
zen hinaus bekannt und be-
liebt. Auch außerhalb
Deutschlands erfahren die
Liebhaber von „Badischem
Schneckensüpple" und
„Schäufele mit Kartoffel- und Nüsslisalat", wie diese Ge-
richte authentisch zubereitet werden.

Original sächsisch –
The Best of Saxon Food
von Reinhard Lämmel,
96 Seiten, deutsch/englisch,
ISBN 978-3-7750-0494-7.
Authentische Rezepte aus
dem Genussland an der Elbe,
garniert mit kleinen Anekdo-
ten und Informationen über
Historie und sächsische Küchen-
kultur. Ob „Leipziger Allerley",
„vogtländische Schusterpfan-
ne", „sächsisches Gartenhuhn"
oder „Leipziger Lerchen" und „Streuselkuchen zum Ditschen"
– in diesem Buch sind die besten Originalgerichte zu-
sammengestellt.

Original Bayrisch –
The Best of Bavarian Food
von Josef Thaller, 64 Seiten,
deutsch/englisch,
ISBN 978-3-7750-0478-7.
Wer liebt sie nicht, diese urige
Gemütlichkeit der bayrischen
Biergärten und Gaststuben!
An den Orten traditionellen
Genießens gehören Speziali-
täten wie „Weißwurst",
„Brez'n", „Pichelsteiner" oder
„Strauben" einfach dazu.
Nun können diese bodenstän-
digen Gerichte auch zuhause
zubereitet werden.

Original Schwäbisch –
The Best of Swabian Food
von Hermine Kiehnle und
Monika Graff, 77 Seiten,
deutsch/englisch,
ISBN 3-7750-0386-X.
Nicht nur Schwaben lieben
schwäbische Spezialitäten!
Hier steht, wie „Linsen,
Spätzle und Saiten", „Maul-
taschen", „Gaisburger
Marsch" oder „Hefezopf"
original zubereitet werden.
Freunde von Trollinger
und Zwiebelrostbraten können nun ihre Lieblingsgerichte
zuhause servieren.

Original Pfälzisch –
The Best of Palatine Food
von Matthias Mangold und
Monika Graff, 76 Seiten,
deutsch/englisch,
ISBN 3-7750-0471-8.
In der sonnenverwöhnten
Pfalz wächst und gedeiht vie-
les: Wein, Obst, Spargel,
„Keschte" (Esskastanien) und
„Grumbeere" (Kartoffeln), ja
sogar Feigen. Ebenso vielfältig
und abwechslungsreich ist
auch die Küche der Pfalz.

Aus Deutschlands Küchen
von Horst Scharfenberg,
775 Seiten,
ISBN 978-3-7750-0415-2.
Quer durch Deutschland, von
Schleswig-Holstein bis Bayern,
vom Saarland bis Sachsen und
Thüringen, werden Original-
rezepte aus allen Regionen vor-
gestellt, sorgfältig recherchiert
aus alten Kochbüchern und
handschriftlichen Notizen.
Eine Fundgrube teilweise fast
vergessener Küchenschätze!

 HÄDECKE

Weitere Informationen über
unsere Kochbücher senden
wir Ihnen gerne zu!

Walter Hädecke Verlag
Postfach 1203
71256 Weil der Stadt

Telefon: +49(0)7033/138080
Telefax: +49(0)7033/1380813
E-Mail: info@haedecke-verlag.de
www.haedecke-verlag.de